COGNITIVE-BEHAVIORAL RELAXATION TRAINING

A New System of Strategies
for Treatment and Assessment

Jonathan C. Smith, Ph.D., has been Professor of Psychology at Chicago's Roosevelt University since 1976 and is currently Director of the University's Stress Institute. In addition, Dr. Smith maintains a small private practice, consults for business and health organizations, and frequently conducts workshops and training programs. Dr. Smith's specialty is relaxation training, meditation, and stress assessment and management. His previous books include *Relaxation Dynamics: A Cognitive-Behavioral Approach to Relaxation* and *Meditation: A Sensible Guide to a Timeless Discipline.* Dr. Smith received his undergraduate degree from Oberlin College and his doctorate from Michigan State University in 1975.

COGNITIVE-BEHAVIORAL RELAXATION TRAINING

A New System of Strategies for Treatment and Assessment

Jonathan C. Smith, Ph.D.

Springer Publishing Company
New York

Copyright © 1990 by Jonathan C. Smith, Ph.D.

Published by Springer Publishing Company

Springer Publishing Company, Inc.
536 Broadway
New York, NY 10012

90 91 92 93 94 / 5 4 3 2 1

ISBN 0-8261-7070-6

Printed in the United States of America

To the quilt.
So many names. So many friends.

Contents

Contents

Preface

Is Another Approach to Relaxation Really Necessary?

Health professionals have at their disposal a profusion of relaxation procedures. Is another approach really necessary? Cognitive-behavioral relaxation training offers something new—a conceptual and practical framework for integrating the technique options available today. It is a *metasystem* that respects the uniqueness of separate approaches and avoids superficial reductionism (everything is hypnosis, the relaxation response, attentional diversion, etc.). Above all, cognitive-behavioral relaxation training is designed to be highly individualized and practical, in the tradition of cognitive-behavior therapy (Beck, 1976; Ellis & Grieger, 1977; Kelly, 1955; Meichenbaum 1977).

Cognitive-behavior therapy is based on the premise that behavior can be changed through the systematic application of scientifically derived learning principles. Emphasis is placed on assessing and modifying maladaptive and irrational cognitions, that is, ways of viewing oneself and the world. In cognitive-behavior therapy, therapist and client are active collaborators, working together toward mutually agreed upon goals.

Cognitive-behavior relaxation training is based on the following premises:

1. Different approaches to relaxation have different effects and work for different people.

2. The best way to teach relaxation is not to impose one or two approaches on everyone, but to introduce a variety of approaches and develop an individualized relaxation sequence tailored to client needs and goals.
3. The goal of relaxation training goes beyond the relaxation response of lowered arousal. Additional objectives are developing cognitive skills of focusing, passivity, and receptivity and acquiring cognitive structures, that is, beliefs, values, and commitments conducive to deepening relaxation and extending its rewards to all of life.

This book outlines the theory and procedural specifics of cognitive-behavioral relaxation training. Chapter 1 argues that the prevailing model underlying most relaxation theory and practice is seriously flawed and that it is time to look at relaxation in a new way. Chapter 2 introduces the conceptual bases for cognitive-behavioral relaxation training, tracing its roots to the transactional model of stress and cognitive-behavioral approaches to psychotherapy. Chapter 3 takes a broader look at the course of relaxation and the assessment of depth. In Chapter 4 we see how the hundreds of approaches to relaxation available to health professionals are not interchangeable, but form a hierarchy of nine distinct clusters. Chapters 5 and 6 review cognitive-behavioral procedures now available and suggest ways of evaluating the "coherence" and "integrity" of a relaxation program. We conclude with the observation that relaxation training is both a science and an art. Its dual goals include carefully trying and testing out various techniques, and then constructing a relaxation program with structure and meaning.

This book is designed for a wide audience, including psychologists, social workers, counselors, nurses, rehabilitation specialists, and psychiatrists. It is directed toward the practitioner already trained in relaxation as well as the student. However, it is not a self-help book or procedural manual of specific exercises. Readers who desire additional instruction in relaxation are advised to consult Smith (1989, 1986).

Finally, I cannot emphasize too much that the model and instructions presented in this book are intended as *extended hypotheses*, not proven facts. To enhance readability, I have chosen not to precede every hypothesis with the phrase: "It is hypothesized."

CHAPTER 1

The Contemporary Model of Relaxation: A Critique

Relaxation is perhaps the most applied, and least understood, clinical tool. Over the decades, a burgeoning catalog of techniques has evolved, including autogenic training, deep breathing, hypnosis, imagery, Lamaze, meditation, progressive relaxation, yoga, Zen, and so on (Appendix A). And yet there is no workable system for selecting, comparing, or even just making sense out of what is available. Clinicians face the temptation of narrowly adhering to one relaxation approach, ignoring others assumed to be equally effective. All of this while the practitioner, lacking professional guidance, faces a cacaphony of claims from cults, religions, and popular psychology.

Much of the present state of affairs can be traced to a perspective that has been dominant for over half a century: relaxation is reduced arousal. A client who can lower heart rate, blood pressure, breathing rate, muscle tension, and the like has learned to relax. In this book I argue that, in spite of its intuitive appeal, the arousal reduction model has reached the limits of its usefulness. It is time to view, teach, and practice relaxation in a new way.

THE AROUSAL REDUCTION MODEL

In the early 1970s, Benson and his colleagues (Wallace, Benson, & Wilson, 1971; Wallace & Benson, 1972) found that practitioners of transcendental meditation (TM), a popular relaxation technique in the 1970s, show a constellation of physiological changes suggesting deepened

1

relaxation (decreased heartrate, blood pressure, respiration rate, brain wave activity, etc.). This research was not only partly responsible for making TM one of the most popular relaxation techniques of the decade, but popularized arousal reduction, specifically the phrase "relaxation response," as a definition of relaxation.

The idea underlying the arousal reduction model is simple. Humans have an inherited potential for relaxation that is the antithesis of Cannon's (Cannon, 1932) emergency fight-or-flight stress response. This response is a constellation of physiological changes, mediated by the sympathetic nervous system, that automatically prepare the organism to respond to threat with vigorous physical or emotional activity. In contrast, the relaxation response, mediated primarily by the parasympathetic system, automatically results in a protective reduction in arousal.

Benson's popularized notions are actually preceded by the work of W. R. Hess. In 1925 Hess began an ambitious exploration of the diencephalon, a project which won him the 1949 Nobel Prize. His experiments (Hess, 1957), performed on 350 cats, localized various autonomic functions such as blood pressure, respiration, micturition, defecation, and sleep. Hess discovered that electrically stimulating certain areas in the diencephalon (principally the thalamus and hypothalamus) consistently resulted in different behaviors, grouped along an "ergotropic-trophotropic" and sympathetic-parasympathetic dimension. Ergotropic responses are oriented toward increased metabolism and utilization of energy, as in Cannon's fight-or-flight response. In contrast, the trophotropic response is characterized by generalized reductions in arousal, presumably to protect the organism against "overstress" and promote restorative processes.

Strictly physiological functions can be elicited through stimulation of centers below the diencephalon. These in turn appear to be integrated with behavior in the diencephalon proper. It is in the diencephalon that lowered blood pressure, decreased respiration rate, and so on, become associated with (in cats) making postural adjustments, seeking a comfortable position, reclining, lowering the head, closing the eyes, and settling into sleep. Indeed, Hess called this pattern the "hypnogenic effect," establishing a parallel with human relaxation. Although Hess triggered the trophotropic response directly through electrical stimulation, the mediating role of the diencephalon suggests that behavioral modifications, such as practicing a relaxation exercise, might have the same effect.

Variations of the arousal reduction model have appeared over the years with slightly differing points of emphasis. Autogenic training theorists (Luthe, 1969–1973) have focused on the effect of autonomic phrases on reducing stimulus input and evoking parallel physiological changes. Jacobson (1938) speculated that reduced stimulation from skeletal muscles in turn lowers cortical and autonomic arousal. Gellhorn (1967) has suggested that repeated practice of relaxation results in a lowered threshold and stronger magnitude of the trophotropic response, termed "trophotropic tuning." Finally, Ornstein (1972) has proposed that reduced and unchanging stimulus input results in diffuse habituation of dominant (verbal) hemisphere functioning.

Davidson and Schwartz (1976) have recently proposed a "specific effects" hypothesis, a variation of the arousal reduction model that differentiates somatic and cognitive anxiety. Physical techniques such as progressive relaxation and yoga stretching should reduce physical arousal symptoms, whereas cognitive techniques such as meditation should have more impact on cognitive arousal (uncontrollable thoughts, etc.).

Although some reviewers have commented (Lichstein, 1988; Shapiro, 1980) on what appears to be a surfeit of relaxation theories, in fact most are based on the same idea—relaxation is reduced arousal. Indeed, it is no overstatement that the arousal reduction model has become the universally accepted definition of relaxation—an observation that has been made and lamented by others (Borkovec, Johnson, & Block, 1984; West, 1987). It is the perspective taken by each of the more than 200 textbooks in clinical psychology, behavior therapy, behavioral medicine, clinical social work, and psychiatry that I have reviewed. It is central to all rationales presented in the classic procedural manuals for progressive relaxation, autogenic training, and meditation (Benson, 1975; Jacobson, 1929; Schultz & Luthe, 1959; Wolpe, 1958). Finally, by my count, arousal reduction is the primary dependent variable for 75 to 90% of relaxation studies cited in the most recent and comprehensive reviews (Lichstein, 1988; Shapiro & Walsh, 1984; Smith, 1989; West, 1987; Woolfolk & Lehrer, 1984).

To those who use and teach relaxation, the arousal reduction model may seem beyond question. However, recently biofeedback, meditation, and other popular approaches to relaxation have been the target of a number of seemingly unrelated attacks. In addition, serious inconsistencies exist between how relaxation is traditionally conceptualized and how it is actually taught. Taken together, these problem areas pose a serious challenge to the arousal reduction model.

CHALLENGES TO THE AROUSAL REDUCTION MODEL

The Question of Technique Equivalence

Benson has frequently proposed (1975) that all relaxation techniques are interchangeable since they all evoke the relaxation response. Indeed, research consistently supports this claim (Lichstein, 1988; Shapiro & Walsh, 1984; West, 1987; Woolfolk & Lehrer, 1984). Recent attempts to subdivide arousal, for example, into cognitive and somatic subsystems (Davidson & Schwartz, 1976) imply technique equivalence within subsystems. That is, all somatic techniques, including progressive relaxation and yoga stretching, should be equally effective in reducing somatic arousal, as are cognitive techniques as meditation and imagery in reducing cognitive arousal. However, no matter how arousal is defined or divided, the assumption of technique equivalence has been seriously challenged by prominent relaxation therapists (Lichstein, 1988; Shapiro, 1980; Woolfolk & Lehrer, 1984). Note this observation of Borkovec and Bernstein, authors of a widely-used progressive relaxation manual (Bernstein & Borkovec, 1973):

> For the most part, research findings suggest that the type of technique employed really does not matter; all of the strategies result in rather similar outcomes when groups of subjects are compared. These results do not, however, correspond with the experience of clinicians who use relaxation approaches with their clients. They have found that there are marked individual differences in the effects of different techniques on clients' symptoms and general feeling states. (Borkovec & Bernstein, 1989, p. xi)

This challenge has been most clearly articulated in biofeedback literature. A remarkable series of major reviews have concluded that biofeedback adds nothing to the arousal-reducing potential of shorter and less expensive self-relaxation strategies (Lichstein, 1988; Linton, 1983; Marzuk, 1985; Reed, Katkin, & Goldband, 1987; Silver & Blanchard, 1978). Indeed, some have described biofeedback as a "gimmick" (Roberts, 1985) akin to faddish megavitamin treatments for cancer (Reed, Katkin, & Goldband, 1987). In spite of this evidence, Schneider (1987), in her presidential address to the Biofeedback Society of America, has argued forcefully that clinicians can and do find biofeedback a highly useful adjunct to therapy.

We find the same challenge in yet another relaxation literature. A number of reviews (Shapiro & Walsh, 1984; West 1987; Woolfolk & Lehrer, 1984), have concluded that there are few differences between the effects of meditation and other approaches to relaxation. After examining this evidence, West concluded with a koan, an insolvable meditative riddle or puzzle: Although research fails to find any special effect for meditation, students and teachers of meditation find meditation to be subjectively unique in many ways. This is one of many riddles that lie hidden in relaxation research.

Floor Effect

Research shows that most people can learn to relax in only two to four sessions (Borkovec & Sides, 1979; Lehrer, 1978). Lehrer and Woolfolk (1984) have concluded that the rapidity with which relaxation can be learned makes it difficult to find differences between approaches. However, in contradiction to these studies, normal subjects frequently report increasingly deep and rewarding levels of relaxation even after years of practice (Lichstein, 1988; Shapiro & Walsh, 1984).

Lack of Effect

Perhaps the most serious and aggressive attack on relaxation has been directed toward meditation. Holmes (1984, 1987) has vigorously argued that the arousal-reducing potential of meditation is no better than that of simply sitting and reading, listening to music, or resting and doing nothing. He even likens meditation to blood letting as a method of helping. His conclusions triggered a storm of controversy, resulting in eight extended comments in the *American Psychologist* (Benson & Friedman, 1985; Holmes, 1985a, 1985b, 1987; Shapiro, 1985; Smith, 1986b; Suler, 1985; West, 1985) and even a comment in *The New York Times*. Clinicians using progressive relaxation, biofeedback, or autogenic techniques may have little interest in what may seem to be a debate in a distant, unrelated discipline. However, as we have noted, research generally shows other forms of relaxation to be no better than meditation. Holmes's challenge has serious implications for all relaxation.

Relaxation-Induced Anxiety

Relaxation-induced anxiety may well be the most frequently reported adverse reaction to relaxation training. It is displayed by up to 40% of those who learn relaxation (Heide & Borkovec, 1984); and has been observed for a wide variety of techniques including progressive relaxation, autogenic training, hypnosis, meditation, and imagery. The arousal reduction model permits an interpretation that such anxiety might occur if a technique is applied to the wrong mode of arousal response, for example, a somatic technique for cognitive arousal. Also, as Ley (Ley & Walker, 1973) has suggested, alterations in respiration can contribute to panic-like states in relaxation. Finally, the cognitive-somatic variant of the arousal reduction model permits symptom desynchrony, that is, an increase in arousal in one symptom modality accompanied by a decrease in another. However, advocates of the arousal model have some difficulty explaining why adverse reactions rarely occur to more than one technique (Heide & Borkovec, 1984), or outlining the processes that enable some relaxers to report deep relaxation, while at the same time display increased arousal (Corby et al., 1978; Lazarus & Folkman, 1984; Shapiro, 1980; West, 1987; Woolfolk, 1975).

Failure to Explain Popular Sequences

The most significant commonality among prominent relaxation programs may be their reliance on combinations of exercises rather than a single technique. Furthermore, exercise combinations are typically presented in a similar order. As seen in Table 1.1, most sequences start with progressive relaxation or stretching exercises, proceed to breathing and imagery, and end with meditation.

Of course, the preference of virtually all seasoned relaxation trainers may be unwarranted; single technique, one-modality approaches could be more effective than any sequence. However, if the practitioners prove to be right, the arousal reduction model cannot account for their preference, other than to suggest that reductions in muscle tension may be conducive to fostering images (Wolpe, 1958) or practicing a cognitive technique. There is no clear reason why autogenic suggestions should precede mental imagery (Luthe, 1977; Stroebel, 1983), progressive relaxation or yoga stretching come before deep breathing exercises (Budzynski, 1974; Charlesworth & Nathan, 1982; Iyengar, 1965; Rama, Ballentine, & Ajaya, 1976) or breathing exercises before cognitive techniques (Benson, 1975; Budzynski, 1974; Charlesworth & Nathan, 1982; Iyengar, 1965; Kapleau, 1965; Patel, 1984; Rama, Ballentine, & Ajaya, 1976). Perhaps there is a lesson to be learned from those who have devoted their lives to teaching and practicing relaxation.

TABLE 1.1 Exercise Sequences for Popular Approaches to Self-Relaxation

Autogenic Training (Luthe, 1977)
  Limb warmth and heaviness suggestions
  Other somatic relaxation suggestions (abdomen, heart, forehead)
  Somatic imagery
  "Meditation" (imagery)

Benson's Breathing One Meditation (Benson, 1975)
  Muscle relaxation
  Slow breathing
  Meditation

Brief Progressive Relaxation (Bernstein & Borkovec, 1973)
  Tense-let go exercises
  Somatic imagery ("recall what it was like to release muscles")

Quieting Reflex Training (Stroebel, 1983)
  Breathing exercises
  Tense-let go exercises
  Limb warmth and heaviness suggestions
  Other somatic relaxation suggestions (abdomen, forehead)
  Mental imagery

Relaxation Training Program (Budzynski, 1974)
  Tense-let go exercises
  Breathing exercises
  Limb warmth and heaviness suggestions

Relaxation Training Sequence (Charlesworth & Nathan, 1982)
  Tense-let go exercises
  Breathing exercises
  Limb warmth and heaviness suggestions
  Other somatic relaxation suggestions (abdomen, heart, forehead)
  Mental imagery

Yoga (Iyengar, 1965; Rama, Ballentine, & Ajaya, 1976)
  Yoga stretching
  Breathing exercises
  Meditation

Yoga Therapy (Patel, 1984)
  Breathing exercises
  Limb warmth and heaviness suggestions
  Meditation

Zen Meditation Training (Kapleau, 1965)
  Breathing exercises
  Somatic abdominal relaxation suggestions (optional)
  Meditation

THE AROUSAL REDUCTION MODEL AND RELAXATION TRAINING

Perhaps the most serious problem with the arousal reduction model is that it tempts one to view relaxation simply in terms of symptom relief, divorced from the broader context of therapy, and indeed of life itself. It is no coincidence that clinicians frequently describe relaxation procedures as the "aspirin" of therapy (Russo, Bird, & Masek, 1980). Similarly, the arousal reduction model makes relaxation somewhat analogous with physical fitness training. Workshops on yoga, progressive relaxation, and meditation fit well in today's health clubs; one rides an exercycle to improve the heart, lifts weights to build chest muscles, and practices progressive relaxation to reduce muscle tension. Relaxation is little more than a whirlpool bath, good for a splash, and then left behind.

Perhaps such reductionism is one price we pay for secularizing techniques that can be traced to magic and religion (Appendix A). However, there is an important difference between endorsing a specific dogma of centuries past and affirming a client's responsibilities to choose what in life is real, important, and worthy of action. It is my thesis that such choices, rather than the reduction of arousal, are what make relaxation work. In the next chapter we begin to present a new view of relaxation, one that not only respects the diversity of approaches now available, but sees relaxation as part of a broader context of life's actions, beliefs, values, and commitments.

CHAPTER 2

A Cognitive-Behavioral Model of Relaxation

THE TRANSACTIONAL MODEL AND COGNITIVE-BEHAVIOR THERAPY

The prevailing arousal reduction model of relaxation is not so much incorrect as it is incomplete. An important parallel can be found in biological, medical, and to some extent, psychological research on stress. We noted earlier that Cannon (1932) defined stress as a fight-or-flight response, a constellation of physiological changes that prepare one for vigorous emergency action. More than a decade after Cannon, Hans Selye (1956) elaborated by proposing three phases of stress reaction: (a) alarm and mobilization (in which physiological resources are aroused and called into action), (b) resistance (physiological adaptation is at its peak), and (c) exhaustion and disintegration (resources are depleted and the organism loses its ability to resist further threat). The definitions of stress proposed by Cannon and Selye became widely accepted and by 1956 the arousal perspective prevailed in nearly 6 thousand publications a year (Appley & Trumbull, 1967).

For over two decades, Richard Lazarus and his colleagues have pointed out the inadequacies of viewing stress as a response. First, this approach does not tell us prospectively when a stimulus, whether it be a major life event or minor hassle, will be stressful or not; we must wait for the reaction. Second, arousal in itself may or may not stress related. For example, a jogger may experience elevations in heart and breathing rate and still feel deeply relaxed and at peace. Thus, the central flaw of

9

the arousal response definition of stress is its circularity: arousal is stress-related only if it follows certain stimuli; a stimulus is stressful only if it triggers arousal. Lazarus (Lazarus, 1966; Lazarus & Folkman, 1984) has proposed an alternative definition of stress that has become widely accepted among researchers: stress is a transactional process involving arousal as well as external stimuli, coping resources, and cognitive appraisal. Most important, to understand stress, we must examine a person's cognitions. This perspective solves the intrinsic limitations of the response model and enables us to view stress as an active, dynamic process that is unique for every individual.

Whereas the transactional model of stress is the product of research-oriented psychologists, cognitive-behavior therapy grew out of the clinic. Early approaches to behavior therapy were primarily based on the stimulus-response psychology of Pavlov (1927), Hull (1943), and Skinner (1938) and focused on modifying overt behavior through the direct application of classical and operant conditioning. For example, a therapist might seek to objectively alter maladaptive reinforcement contingencies, pair relaxation exercises with phobic stimuli, and so on. More recently (Bandura, 1969), cognitive-behavior therapists have focused on intermediary cognitions such as perceptions, expectations, beliefs. Theoretically, classical conditioning is no longer viewed as an automatic reflexive process; instead, conditioned responses are self-activated on the basis of learned cognitions. Similarly, reinforcement is not so much an automatic strengthener of behavior, but a source of information and incentive that regulates behavior. In practice, Ellis's rational emotive therapy (Ellis & Grieger, 1977), directs treatment to restructuring basic irrational beliefs central to a client's problems, while Beck (1976) and Meichenbaum (1977) have placed somewhat more importance on modifying maladaptive cognitions. Although the relative merit of stimulus-response and cognitive-behavioral approaches to therapy is still debated, the cognitive-behavioral approach has emerged as the more popular of the two. It has the advantage of offering the clinician additional flexibility without abandoning tools derived from traditional operant or classical conditioning.

It is ironic that neither the transactional nor cognitive-behavioral models have been applied extensively to relaxation, often viewed as the opposite of the stress and a widely used tool in the health professions. In fact, these models suggest there is more to relaxation than the relaxation response. Furthermore, they prompt us to take an individualized approach and question the value of applying variations of the same technique to all clients. Finally, the transactional and cognitive-behavioral models place central importance on personal experimentation and trial and error in dealing with the stressors and problems of living. As we shall see in the chapters to come, it is this emphasis that prompts us to view relaxation, not as a mechanical and static chore, but as a dynamic and continuing adventure.

A COGNITIVE-BEHAVIORAL MODEL OF RELAXATION

Our cognitive-behavioral model of relaxation does not reject the importance of arousal, but puts it in perspective. It should not be seen so much as proven fact, but as an extended hypothesis, a challenge to relaxation researchers and practitioners to look beyond a perspective that is in crisis. We begin with a consideration of cognitive processes and structures.

Cognitive Processes

Cognitive processes are the ways one assimilates information. Stress researchers have focused on how people selectively seek, attend to, and recall information. In addition, cognitive-behavioral clinicians have introduced a variety of cognitive restructuring processes, for example, exploring and testing the utility and veracity of maladaptive beliefs, values, and commitments (Meichenbaum, 1985; Beck, 1976; Ellis, 1962). Our model begins with the following general hypothesis:

> Three cognitive processes are basic to relaxation: focusing, the ability to identify, differentiate, maintain attention on, and return attention to simple stimuli for an extended period, passivity, the ability to stop unnecessary goal-directed and analytic activity, and receptivity, the ability to tolerate and accept experiences that may be uncertain, unfamiliar, or paradoxical (Smith, 1989).

These basic processes are what make all relaxation work. For example, the following hypothetical vignettes illustrate casual, everyday relaxation:

> One day I was doing my housework. Everything was happening at once—the TV was on, the kids were playing outside, the upstairs neighbors were playing loud music, and so on. I was getting very tense and decided I needed a rest. I went to my quiet den, closed the door, took the phone off the hook, and told myself "For the next few

minutes I'm going ignore all the distractions and attend to one thing—reading my favorite magazine."

I was getting really tense over my job. Everything seemed like it had to be done at once. I was being pulled in a hundred directions at once, first to answer the phone, then work on a report, then answer a letter. Finally I said to myself "Look, take it easy. Relax. Do one thing at a time and let everything else be."

After studying a few hours I like to rest on my couch and close my eyes. I let a pleasant fantasy of some distant tropical island go through my mind. One day, I began to feel like I was floating. This was a new and strange sensation and I almost got up and called the doctor. However, I then decided that these feelings are OK, just a sign that I am relaxing. Now I even pretend I am floating when I'm relaxing.

The person who thinks "I'm going to ignore all the distractions" has, in a simple way, decided to focus. In the second example, the statement "Do one thing at a time" represents a decision to let go and take a more passive stance toward the world. Finally, the student who realizes that his sensations of floating are "OK, just a sign that I am relaxing" has learned to be more receptive and tolerate experiences that may at first seem uncertain, unfamiliar, or paradoxical.

These same skills, focusing, passivity, and receptivity, are present when one engages in formal relaxation training. For example, in contemporary versions of progressive relaxation one: (1) focuses on and discriminates sensations of tension and tension release, (2) overtly, and then covertly, lets go and becomes passive after generating tension, and (3) tolerates temporary boredom, frustration, and discomfort until relaxation skills begin to develop (Bernstein & Borkovec, 1973). Practitioners of all forms of relaxation, whether it be autogenic training, breathing, or Zen, are essentially doing the same thing—honing and refining their ability to attend to a limited stimulus; ceasing unnecessary goal-directed and analytic activity; and tolerating and accepting experiences that may be uncertain, unfamiliar, and paradoxical.

As relaxation training progresses, focusing, passivity, and receptivity change in an important way. At first these skills are utilized concretely; one simply attends to and lets go of tension with a certain open mind. However, as one becomes more proficient at relaxation, skills are deployed in increasing degrees of abstraction or generality. Focusing can become a small act of dedication, of deciding to deploy one's attention in relaxation in spite of the impulse to do otherwise. Passivity can be viewed as an act of letting be, of relinquishing unnecessary control.

Receptivity can become an expression of hope or faith in rewards yet unseen. In order for this to happen, certain structures conducive to relaxation must begin to develop.

Cognitive Structures

Cognitive structures are the beliefs, values, and commitments that underlie thoughts, speech, and actions. They represent our enduring ideas concerning what is real and important as well as our choices concerning various courses of action. Structures serve to help us quickly identify, categorize, and interpret stimuli; fill in missing information; obtain further information; solve a problem; and reach a goal (Markus, 1977). In addition, they define the depth and breadth of relaxation. However, structures are hypothetical constructs and cannot be seen. They exert much of their influence through and receive much of their support from *affirming* thought, speech, and action.

Our second hypothesis focuses on the role of restructuring in relaxation:

> *The central task of relaxation is to relinquish structures and associated nonaffirming behavior incompatible with relaxation, and acquire and affirm structures conducive to continued and deepened relaxation.*

For example, examine the following internal dialogue of a student having trouble with progressive relaxation:

> Wasting time with relaxation will drain me of energy; relaxation is laziness; I have decided to devote every available minute to productive activity.

Such nonaffirming thoughts reveal an implicit belief that relaxation is incompatible with activity, a low valuing of relaxation, and a commitment to actions inconsistent with relaxation. Once such structures change, our student is more likely to experience success at progressive relaxation. In contrast, this more affirming internal dialogue suggests that relaxation is beginning to work:

> It feels nice to squeeze and let go of muscle tension. I think my technique is a good way of reducing stress. I plan to continue practicing.

When our student has decided that his relaxation experiences are real, important, and worthy of action, he has acquired structures supportive of relaxation. He has, at least in the context of the relaxation session, changed and replaced a small belief, value, or commitment so that relaxation may proceed.

In time, increasingly abstract structures begin to develop. Relatively restricted attitudes evolve into more encompassing personal philosophies (Table 2.1). For example, the thought that "It's good to let go of needless muscle tension" can be seen as part of a concrete value that recognizes that relaxation has some, although limited, worth. Later, this value may become more abstract, that is, a realization that "It's good to let go of needless attempts to control all things in life."

In addition, relaxation structures become increasingly differentiated as implications and applications are spelled out and experientially validated. The philosophy "Flow with the present" is little more than a slogan until its concrete ramifications are articulated ("It is senseless to become preoccupied with worries about yesterday's argument with the boss . . . It is useless to try to do everyone's job for them . . . I will just have to accept that it may be impossible to predict what my boss will think of my suggestion, etc."). As we shall see later, structure abstraction/differentiation may be an important variable determining the depth of relaxation one can achieve and the degree to which relaxation generalizes to life at large (Lichstein, 1988; Shapiro, 1984; Smith, 1986a).

However, so far our hypothesized model does not explain how processes and structures change in relaxation. How does the relaxing client develop skill at focusing, passivity and receptivity? What is it that enables increasingly abstract and differentiated structures to develop? How do beliefs, values, and commitments interfere with or contribute to relaxation training? To answer these questions we need to take a deeper look relaxation processes and structures, beginning, as we did earlier, with the subjective experience of relaxation.

The Skill-Mastery Cycle

Hassles and Uplifts

As discussed in Chapter 1, relaxation-induced anxiety is known to be a frequent side effect of relaxation training. To borrow a term from the transactional model of stress, such reactions are some of the "hassles" of relaxation (Delongis, Coyne, Dakof, Folkman, & Lazarus, 1982; Kanner, Coyne, Schaefer, & Lazarus, 1981; Lazarus & Folkman, 1984). According to the arousal reduction model, relaxation-induced anxiety can be an undesired symptom, a sign of a mismatch of technique and problem.

TABLE 2.1 Examples of Concrete and Abstract Cognitive Structures

Structures Supporting Distraction

Concrete

Beliefs

"Pursuing a worry during a relaxation session will help me solve it."

"Relaxation isn't working unless it produces a dramatic 'high' or altered state."

"If I relax too much, I might lose control."

Values

"Productive worry during a relaxation session is valuable."

"Sitting still, even if it feels good, is nothing more than an idle waste of time."

"Relaxation exercises take too long to work."

Commitments

"Whenever a relaxation session is interrupted by a worrisome concern that feels important, I choose to pursue the worry."

"I'll practice my relaxation exercise whenever I have nothing better to do."

"I've decided to practice relaxation while watching TV."

Abstract

Beliefs

"The most effective route to health and success is to strive to be perfect in all things."

"I am not capable of making my life better."

"Things will automatically get better on their own."

Values

"I place high importance on perfect health, and being successful in everything I pursue."

"I do not feel good about myself when I am less than totally successful at work or school."

"Unless others love and accept me, I can't feel at peace with myself."

Commitments

"I choose to work my absolute hardest at everything I do."

"If something threatens my current routine, I just won't pay any attention to it."

"I always strive to make a good impression on others."

Structures Supporting Relaxation

Concrete

Beliefs

"The muscle relaxation I feel during a relaxation session may enable me to have a less stressful day."

TABLE 2.1 *(continued)*

Structures Supporting Relaxation

Concrete

"Relaxation may be working, even during sessions that may not feel productive."

"The warmth and heaviness I feel in relaxation are normal signs that my body is beginning to relax."

Values

"Because the muscle relaxation I feel is enjoyable, I value it as important."

"I am now beginning to treasure my time off periods as important time just for myself."

"I'm proud of the fact that I'm beginning to develop relaxation skills."

Commitments

"I have decided to do my muscle relaxation exercise every day."

"I will not eat, smoke, or drink coffee before practicing relaxation."

"I plan to complete my relaxation session, even if it begins to get a bit boring."

Abstract

Beliefs

"My selfish worries are distractions that fog awareness of a deeper reality."

"God loves me and has a plan for my life."

"The meaning of life becomes more apparent to me in the quiet of relaxation."

Values

"My urgent concerns seem less important when seen in broader perspective."

"There are more important things than my everyday hassles."

"At the deepest level I can feel at peace with myself—I am an OK person."

Commitments

"I choose to live one day at a time and not worry about things that cannot be changed."

"I choose to quit creating unnecessary pain and tension for myself by ignoring my true feelings."

"God's will be done."

However, seasoned relaxation instructors frequently have a different understanding. For teachers of autogenic training, such symptoms reflect potentially therapeutic autogenic discharges (Luthe, 1977). In hypnosis they may reflect abreactive or uncovering processes (Reyher, 1964). In clinically standardized as well as Zen meditation, anxiety can be a sign of unstressing, normalization, and stress release (Carrington, 1978; Ikemi, Ishikawa, Goyeche, & Sasaki, 1978). Each of these notions implies that the hassles of relaxation are not so much problems as indicators that a technique is working. They are, as Lichstein (1988) has put it, "blessed irritants." More formally, relaxation appears to unearth potentially distracting sources of anxiety and dealing with such anxiety somehow contributes to further relaxation.

According to the transactional model of stress, everyday hassles have an equally important counterpart, satisfying and enjoyable experiences known as "uplifts" (Delongis et al., 1982; Kanner et al., 1981; Lazarus & Folkman, 1984). So to, every approach to relaxation has its uplifts, rewarding experiences associated with lowered arousal and increased focusing, passivity, and receptivity. Such experiences can range from an absence of muscle tension, to feelings of "warmth and heaviness," to pleasurable imagery, and even ecstatic meditative states. Uplifts play a role similar to the hassles of relaxation; both imply a cyclical skill mastery process central to all relaxation.

In cognitive-behavioral terms, the practitioner of relaxation experiences cycles of decreased and increased arousal, focusing, passivity, and receptivity. This cycle can be described in terms of convergent and divergent processes.[1]

Convergent Processes

By directing attention to a limited stimulus, reducing goal-directed and analytic activity, and remaining receptive to effects that may be uncertain, unfamiliar, or paradoxical, one sets into motion a convergent cycle in which cognitive and somatic activity are reduced and focusing, passivity, and receptivity are enhanced.

A variety of general subordinate processes may contribute to this hypothesized phase of the cycle. By simply diverting attention from outside stimuli and tasks, as well as thought and worry, the relaxer removes an important source of distraction and arousal. One is simply less likely to think about stimuli that do not occupy the center of attention (Ellis, 1984). Similarly, attending to the relaxation task reduces

[1] As we explore this cycle, it is important not to be preoccupied by the potentially bewildering array of subordinate processes that may contribute to convergent and divergent phases. Many additional processes not listed here may be involved and some we have suggested may prove to be unimportant; all too often relaxation researchers have attempted to define all of relaxation in terms of one subordinate process. As Lichstein has noted, an adequate theory of relaxation must somehow summon a range of views, each capturing a unique, indispensable facet of a multivariate phenomenon (Lichstein, 1988, p. 44). Our relaxation cycle can be seen as both a model of relaxation, and an organizing tool for conceptualizing a diverse array of limited-domain theories.

the amount of attentional capacity left for somatically or cognitively arousing stimuli (Davidson & Schwartz, 1976). In addition, arousal may be further reduced by a variety of exercise-specific subordinate processes, for example, the relaxation rebound of each progressive relaxation tension-release cycle (Bernstein & Borkovec, 1973), or decreased oxygenation from certain breathing exercises (Lichstein, 1988).

As one continues the systematic practice of relaxation, a variety of long-term processes may contribute to further reductions in arousal and increments in skill development (Smith, 1989). Put briefly, through desensitization, distractions once associated with tension and arousal eventually become linked with relaxation and are less likely to be disruptive (Goleman, 1971). In addition, blocking the act of pursuing distraction deprives such acts of potential reinforcement. In the absence of reinforcement, such acts are more likely to extinguish (Smith, 1989). Finally, the practitioner of relaxation tends to experience habituation of reactions appraised as unimportant, continuous, and unchanging (Ornstein, 1972). Although other long-term convergent processes no doubt can be identified, desensitization, extinction, and habituation have been most frequently mentioned in the relaxation literature.

Divergent Processes

Divergent processes interfere with arousal reduction, focusing, passivity, and receptivity and provide an opportunity for skill development.

I hypothesize that a variety of factors can lead to an end to convergent movement. These include: discomfort associated with performing an exercise (an unfamiliar relaxation position, relaxation-related twitches, mild hyperventilation from deep breathing, and so on), symptoms related to lowered somatic arousal (feelings of warmth, decreased heartrate, palmar perspiration), novel experiences related to possible shifts in hemispheric dominance (Ornstein, 1972), distractions unearthed because of attentional shifts (Smith, 1989), and potentially disruptive associations to relaxation (Heide & Borkovec, 1984).

Such episodes of increased arousal and distraction place new demands on the relaxer and provide an opportunity to further develop focusing, passivity, and receptivity. Indeed, part of the "work" of relaxation is redeploying relaxation skills after phases of distraction. As a practice effect, skill at deploying focusing, passivity, and receptivity deepens. However, as skills are developing, another cognitive relaxation cycle is operating.

The Cognitive Restructuring Cycle

As relaxation progresses, increasingly abstract and differentiated beliefs, values, and commitments conducive to relaxation are established.

I hypothesize that cognitive restructuring is a central part of relaxation. To understand how this happens, we need to consider how divergent structures supporting distraction are relinquished, and convergent structures supporting focusing, passivity, and receptivity are acquired. This process of restructuring begins when one *articulates*, or identifies and finds labels (words or pictures) for, an experience of tension or relaxation. To explain, let us begin with an example.

Divergent Restructuring

A student of yoga is having some difficulty practicing. Her problem is that her practice session is frequently interrupted by a variety of thoughts. For example, in one session she might think:

> I start practicing and almost at once have the urge to snack. I go ahead and eat. This little diversion is minor and can't hurt my yoga practice. Anyway, I just *can't* resist a good snack. Food is really important for me. I'll do better at staying with my practice tomorrow.

Such thoughts represent more than simple hassles associated with practicing yoga. First, our student has articulated a divergent experience (a snacking impulse). In addition, she has revealed a variety of structures not conducive to continued relaxation. For example, her beliefs appear to include the notion that yoga will work even when not practiced and that she is incapable of resisting distracting snacking impulses. She clearly values food, and has made a commitment to act promptly on snacking impulses.

In time, our yoga student progresses to the point where she can complete and enjoy each practice session. Her self-statements now affirm structures more conducive to relaxation:

> I still have snacking impulses while practicing yoga. However, whether it is the urge for a hamburger, candy bar, or dish of ice cream, I know I am capable of refraining until the end of my session. Constantly interrupting my yoga sessions keeps me from benefitting. It is important for me to stick with my exercise.

Note that structures that initially interfered with practice have been relinquished or modified. More important, her new structures are sufficiently abstract and differentiated to permit continued practice in face of an entire category of articulated distractions, that is, a variety of snacking impulses such as the desire to have a candy bar, hamburger, and so on. However, other distractions not encompassed by the category "snacking impulse" ("My interpersonal needs are so great, I can't resist talking to a friend") may emerge, interrupt the deepening of relaxation, and trigger a divergent phase of the relaxation cycle. Once such impulses are articulated, and their associated beliefs, values, and commitments restructured, our student has increased the number of distractions she can tolerate, and the deepening of relaxation can continue.

To continue, the wish to snack, call a friend, engage in sexual fantasy, and listen to music are all concrete examples of an even more abstract class of distraction, the urge to engage in pleasurable diversion. Eventually, our student may face a new challenge: relinquishing or modifying divergent structures sufficiently abstract and differentiated to encompass broad classes of articulated distractions. To illustrate, she may now think:

> I am distracted by the wish to entertain a sexual fantasy. This is another self-indulgence that can deter me from continuing with my relaxation session. At least for this relaxation session, self-indulgent thoughts are resistible and not important. I choose to put them aside.

To summarize, we have seen the following progression of structures: "I am capable of resisting the urge to snack . . . I am capable of resisting the urge to snack and call my friends . . . I am capable of resisting self-indulgent urges." Each structure is made possible by an articulated diversion, each is more abstract and differentiated, and each enables our yoga student to reengage the convergent phase of the relaxation cycle and contend with a larger number of potential distractions.

Convergent Restructuring

We have seen lowered arousal and increased focusing, passivity, and receptivity can be associated with a variety of positive experiences or relaxation "uplifts." Such experiences may well serve to reinforce consistent practice, deployment of relaxation skills, and development of supportive structures. In cognitive-behavioral terms, reinforcements contribute to appraisals that relaxation behaviors are desirable and worth maintaining.

However, once articulated, relaxation uplifts can also contribute to the acquisition of increasingly abstract and differentiated convergent structures. To understand how such convergent restructuring occurs, let us return to our yoga student. After a few weeks of practice, she might identify a variety of "pleasurable muscle stretch sensations." Of course, if she has incompatible structures, and does not believe such sensations are real, value them as important, or chose to accept them, her experiment with yoga will be relatively brief. Once our student acquires supportive structures, she can continue practicing in face of an entire domain of similar articulated stretch sensations (stretching the arms, legs, back, face, and so on). In time, she may identify a variety of other pleasurable somatic relaxation experiences (warmth and heaviness, floating sensations, etc.), requiring a broadening of supportive structures so that deepening may continue. So far, the articulation-restructuring-abstraction process is similar to what we have already encountered, as illustrated by the following four increasingly abstract and differentiated dialogues:

> Arm stretch sensations feel good and may help me deal with the rest of the day more calmly.

> All stretch sensations feel good and may help me deal with the rest of the day more calmly.

> A wide range of soothing body sensations feel good and may help me deal with the rest of the day more calmly.

> An overall sense of physical well-being is desirable and can contribute to a calm that extends through the rest of the day.

In time, a new kind of convergent restructuring may occur. Our student may have to differentiate experiences associated with differing levels of skill deployment. To illustrate, many beginning students report problems with feeling drowsy and falling asleep during a relaxation practice session. For some this may reflect a difficulty in differentiating drowsiness from wakeful relaxation (Smith, 1989), as reflected in the following comment:

> I often fall asleep during mental imagery. That's OK because a small nap can help me deal with stress better.

Once drowsiness and wakeful relaxation are articulated and distinguished, convergent structures supporting drowsiness may have to be modified, as is illustrated below:

> Now I know the difference between sleep and relaxation. If I become drowsy during mental imagery and am truly in need of sleep, I stop

> my session and go to bed. If I am well-rested, I treat my drowsiness
> as a minor distraction, and proceed with imagery. Sleep and imag-
> ery are two different types of relaxation. It is important not to get
> them confused.

Such differentiation and reappraisal can occur at all levels of relaxation. For example, a yoga student may eventually encounter a variety of
somatic sensations, including warmth and heaviness, floating, and so
on, and decide such sensations are important and justify continued
practice. However, as proficiency at focusing, passivity, and receptivity
deepen, she may encounter new convergent experiences potentially in
conflict with established relaxation beliefs, values, and commitments.
For example, she may discover "A pleasurable inner stillness in which
my mind is empty of thought and sensation." Clearly, one cannot value
and seek pleasurable sensation and the pleasurable absence of sensation at the same time; some structural modification must occur in order
to accommodate the new level of skill mastery. She may decide:

> Sensual body pleasures are good at the beginning of practice since
> they help me put aside the hassles of the day and get ready for
> relaxation. However, as relaxation deepens, they become dis-
> tractions, to be calmly put aside.

Notice here that the initial convergent structure is not just relinquished,
but is assimilated into a more encompassing and differentiated structure. If restructuring does not occur, then the new experiences threaten
to interrupt the deepening of relaxation and contribute to divergent
cycle activity.

We can now take a new look at the relaxation cycle. As already
described, cyclical changes in arousal, focusing, passivity, and receptivity may partly represent the deployment and redeployment of relaxation
skills in face of distractions unearthed by divergent processes. Here,
deepening is a practice effect of continued skill redeployment. In broader terms, restructuring introduces a cycle of its own. Relaxation deepens
until experiences are articulated that are not encompassed by existing
structures. Either relaxation terminates or new, increasingly abstract
and differentiated structures, are found (or old ones relinquished) to
support new levels of relaxation. The deepening of relaxation is both a
practice effect and a result of restructuring.

It is important to note that skill mastery and restructuring cycles
interact: Increased levels of skill deployment can call for new structures,
and new structures can bring about distracting divergent experiences
that overwhelm achieved levels of skill mastery. A relaxer capable of

displaying profound levels of passivity may encounter floating sensations requiring a decision whether such sensations are real, important, and worthy of continued practice. A structural change that accepts alterations in body image in relaxation can in itself foster additional related experiences (perceived shrinking, rocking, etc.) that challenge the degree of skill mastery achieved.

Generalization and the Deepening of Relaxation

In broader perspective, increasingly abstract and differentiated structures enable relaxation to generalize outside the practice session. Generalization, in turn, serves to enhance convergent processes contributing to the deepening of relaxation in the practice session. To explain, compare these affirmations of two relaxation students:

> Practicing muscle relaxation is enjoyable and healthy.
>
> Live one moment at a time and let past and future concerns be.

The first statement suggests structures that may increase the likelihood that one will continue practicing and enjoying a specific technique, say progressive relaxation. The second statement may represent a more abstract and differentiated structure that supports not only a relatively focused, passive, and receptive relaxation session, but a more restful stance towards life at large. One can speculate that the relaxer who has successfully acquired the more abstract and differentiated structure is less likely to carry a residue of daily tension into a relaxation practice session, increasing the likelihood of a more deeply relaxing session. Thus, the "work of relaxation" has both *vertical* and *lateral* components, extending the depth of cognitive structures and their breadth to life at large.

Lateral generalization of cognitive structures may well display an abstraction/differentiation process similar to that just outlined. For example, we can think of a relaxer as possessing two classes of beliefs, values, and commitments: *central structures* directly related to the practice of relaxation and *peripheral structures* that apply to life outside of the relaxation session. For example, a relaxer may believe that "daily practice of breathing and imagery exercises helps reduce stress" (central structure) and "a democratic home environment enhances the family" (peripheral structure). Once a relaxer begins to firmly accept central structures, he runs the risk of encountering incompatible peripheral structures that limit the breadth and depth of relaxation. In the meditation session he may believe in taking one thing at a time and "going with the flow," while at work he may display driven behavior based on the implicit philosophy that one must "be in control at all times." The task of relaxation can call for work to be completed outside of the relaxation session. When beliefs, values, and commitments outside of the relaxation session are restructured and affirmed in a way consistent with structures supportive of relaxation, relaxation is further generalized to life at large.

The End Point of Relaxation

What is the final outcome of relaxation? Where does the implied movement of interacting skill mastery and restructuring cycles ultimately lead? In general terms, the outcome is increased skill at focusing, passivity, and receptivity, as well as richly abstract and differentiated relaxation structures generalized to life at large. But, as we shall see in the following chapter, adding any degree of specificity requires asking the practitioner deeply personal and value-laden questions concerning ultimate beliefs, values, and commitments. However, we as scientists need to refrain from advocating any particular philosophical or religious world view. Our role involves taking something of a vow of silence concerning the ultimate end of relaxation, pointing to the process, and respecting each individual's discovered outcome.

Implications of the Cognitive-Behavioral Model

The cognitive-behavioral model we have presented has a number of important implications for treatment. First, the traditional practice of teaching clients one or two relaxation techniques may not be sufficient; the complexity of processes involved in relaxation makes it likely that different approaches work better for different clients and different problems (Chapter 4). In addition, relaxation training must go beyond teaching specific techniques (tensing and letting go, focusing on a meditation stimulus, and so on); additional goals include fostering the acquisition of relaxation skills and structures (Chapters 5 and 6). Although such an approach makes training more complex, it offers a number of important advantages. Since many of the issues considered in therapy are also relevant to the acquisition of appropriate relaxation structures, relaxation can be readily integrated into therapy. In addition, relaxation exercises can be highly individualized, increasing client motivation to practice. Exercises can be firmly linked to basic beliefs, values, and commitments, increasing the salience of relaxation and the likelihood of generalization. Most important, the cognitive-behavioral model makes relaxation instruction a challenging and creative adventure rather than a health chore.

The implications of our model for research are considerable. Most important, the popular strategy of comparing the impact of one or two techniques on a variety of arousal-related dimensions is doomed to obscure relaxation's extensive potential. A thorough assessment of relaxation must include an evaluation of all levels of depth as revealed through the manifestation of focusing, passivity, receptivity, and structure abstraction/differentiation. Indeed, the frequently reported lack of difference among relaxation techniques (Lichstein, 1988; Woolfolk & Lehrer, 1984) may simply be an artifact of inadequate assessment strategies. With this challenge in mind, we now consider the assessment of relaxation.

CHAPTER 3

Assessment and the Path
of Relaxation

What does it mean to be deeply relaxed? What tools are appropriate for assessing relaxation? In terms of our cognitive-behavioral model, different and possibly independent criteria may be appropriate at different times. At the onset of training, it is perhaps more useful to emphasize arousal reduction (indeed, for highly tense individuals, focusing, passivity, and receptivity may correlate highly with arousal). However, as one gains control over arousal, proficiency at deploying focusing, passivity, and receptivity becomes a more useful criterion. Finally, for a client adept at relaxation, an assessment of depth must include an examination of cognitive structures, specifically their degree of abstraction and differentiation, as well as their content and function.

AROUSAL REDUCTION

Reductions in arousal can be manifest in at least three ways: behaviorally, physiologically, or through self-report. Behavioral observation is the least intrusive strategy for assessing depth of relaxation. A variety of potentially useful scales utilize four general categories of indicators (Luiselli, Steinman, Marholin, & Steinman, 1981; Poppen & Maurer, 1982; Smith & Seidel, 1982; Smith, 1989): breathing, posture, muscle activity, and autonomic activity (Table 3.1). Of these, decreased depth and rate of respiration may well be one of the most convenient, reliable, and universal signs (Lichstein, 1988).

A somewhat more intrusive strategy is to assess arousal by means of biofeedback equipment (Table 3.2). In general, biofeedback consists of

Table 3.1 Behavioral Signs of Relaxation Rating Scale

Below are a number of behavioral signs of relaxation. Indicate how well each fits or describes the person you are rating. Do this by putting a number in the space to the left of each statement. Please use the following scale:

How well does the item you are reading fit
the person you are rating?

1 = Fits Not at All
2 = Fits Slightly
3 = Fits Moderately
4 = Fits Very Well
5 = Fits Extremely Well

Breathing

____ 1. Slow breathing pace
____ 2. Even breathing rhythm
____ 3. Greater use of diaphragm (stomach rising and falling)
____ 4. Reduced chest extension

Posture

____ 5. Shoulders sloped
____ 6. Head slightly tilted
____ 7. Limbs and other body parts are in open, relaxed position
      a. Jaws slightly parted
      b. Palms open
      c. Fingers curled and not straight or clenched
      d. Knees and feet pointing apart

Muscle activity

____ 8. Little restless movement
      a. Eyes closed; no blinking, looking around, staring
      b. No fidgeting, tapping, swaying
      c. No chewing, biting lips, swallowing
____ 9. Little clenching and bracing
____ 10. Face, neck, arms, and hands are smooth and unwrinkled with no sign of twitching or extended veins or muscles.

Autonomic activity

____ 11. No stomach noises
____ 12. No throbbing veins
____ 13. No cold hands

Note: Score by adding ratings.
It should be noted that these breathing criteria are somewhat arbitrary since relaxation can affect breathing pattern in different ways. To explain, a tense client may (1) breathe too rapidly or in a way that is forced and slow; (2) take in too much or too little air with each breath; and (3) pause too long or too little between breaths. Thus, relaxation can be reflected in reduced or increased breathing pace, volume, or length of pauses. Research has yet to determine which of these dimensions is most important.

In order to stimulate research on understudied dimensions of relaxation, permission is granted to reproduce this scale for any noncommercial use. All other rights reserved.

27

TABLE 3.2 Frequent Biofeedback Measures

Measures	Physiological Activity Assessed
Electrical	
Electrocardiogram (EKG)	Beating heart
Electrodermal activity (EDA)	Perspiration; emotional sweating
Electroencephalogram (EEG)	Electrical activity of cerebral cortex
Electrogastrogram (EGG)	Stomach contractions
Electromyogram (EMG)	Muscle activity
Electrooculogram (EOG)	Eye movement
Mechanical	
Plethysmograph	Volume of blood flow at a peripheral site; respiration; erectile response
Temperature	Blood volume
Pressure	Blood pressure

Note: Adapted from Reed, Katkin, and Goldband (1987).

measuring and transforming physiological responses into signals that can provide immediate feedback to the client. This information can be used to assist a client in learning to lower arousal. For example, electrical activity associated with muscle tension can be detected through electromyographic equipment. Electrodes might be attached to a target muscle group, for example the frontalis muscle (a muscle in the forehead). A client might then experiment with a variety of relaxation strategies until a desired level of control over arousal is achieved. In actual practice, biofeedback is considerably more complex. Often several responses (for example, muscle tension and temperature, or several target muscle groups) are assessed simultaneously in order to maximize a general relaxation effect (for more on biofeedback, see Peper, Ancoli, & Quinn, 1979; Schwartz, 1987).

Finally, arousal can be assessed through self-report. The simplest procedure is to ask a client to indicate level of relaxation on a 1-to-10 or 1-to-100 "subjective units of distress" scale (Wolpe, 1973). However, a large number of self-report anxiety questionnaires have greater reliability and validity. These generally have three formats: trait ("How do you generally feel?"), recalled state ("How did you feel when relaxing?"), and present state ("How do you feel at the present moment?"). Assessments of present state represent the most direct self-report measures of arousal. Perhaps the most widely used and validated measure of this sort is the State-Trait Anxiety Inventory (Spielberger, Gorsuch, & Lushene, 1970).

Recently, researchers have attempted to differentiate self-report arousal into cognitive and various somatic subdimensions (Borkovec, 1987; Heide & Borkovec, 1983; Schwartz, Davidson, & Goldman, 1978; Smith & Sheridan, 1983). Cognitive arousal inventories tap the degree of unwanted (unimportant or anxiety arousing) thoughts and difficulty controlling thoughts (Weinstein & Smith, 1989). Such inventories are still highly experimental and have yet to be shown to have clinical utility. Stress Inventory-6 (Smith, 1989; Smith & Seidel, 1982; Smith & Sheridan, 1983; Smith & Siebert, 1984) has emerged as a particularly promising measure of self-report somatic arousal (Lichstein, 1988). This scale assesses 18 first-order and 4 second-order factors identified through extensive research of over 1,500 somatic symptoms. (See Table 3.3 for an abbreviated version.)

It should be noted that arousal-based assessments of relaxation have focused primarily on tapping reductions in physical symptomatology. Autogenic therapists (Appendix A) have noted that relaxation can be accompanied by the presence of specific positive somatic sensations such as "warmth and heaviness." In fact, a relatively large number of somatic sensations can serve as signs of increased relaxation (Table 3.4).

It has frequently been noted that behavioral, physiological, and self-report domains of arousal can be independent. For example, one can display rapid heartrate and breathing with few behavioral or self-report signs of tension. Thus, assessments of arousal should ideally tap all three dimensions.

RELAXATION SKILLS

There is little consensus as to the best approach for operationalizing focusing, passivity, and receptivity. Indeed, most researchers and clinicians, because of their adherence to the arousal reduction model, have seen little need to assess cognitive relaxation skills. However, a surprisingly fruitful domain of relaxation research suggests a variety of promising assessment strategies. Since it is likely that few relaxation trainers are aware of this literature, we will examine it in some detail.

With a few exceptions, subjects who respond well to hypnosis or meditation appear to score high on the Tellegen Absorption Scale (Davidson & Schwartz, 1976; Davidson & Goleman, 1977; Curtis, 1984; Heide & Borkovec, 1983, 1984; Norton, Rhodes, & Hauch, 1985; Siebert,

TABLE 3.3 Smith Somatic Stress Symptom Scale

Below are the necessary components for constructing two scales: the Smith Somatic Stress Symptom Scale–State (SSSSS–S) and the Smith Somatic Stress Symptom Scale–Trait (SSSSS–T). To assemble the desired scale (state or trait) combine the appropriate introduction with the 18 items. Delete all bracketed material. To score each scale simply add the item ratings.

[STATE INTRODUCTION]

The following items describe experiences people often have. Please carefully read each and indicate the extent to which it fits you *right now*, at the *present moment*. Rate all the items by putting numbers in the blanks to the left. Use the following key:

How well does the item you are reading fit
how you feel right now, at the present moment?

1 = Fits Me Not at All
2 = Fits Me Slightly
3 = Fits Me Moderately
4 = Fits Me Very Well
5 = Fits Me Extremely Well

[INSERT ITEMS HERE]

[TRAIT INTRODUCTION]

The following items describe experiences people often have. Please read each carefully and indicate the extent to which it fits how you *typically* or *generally* feel. Rate all the items by putting numbers in the blanks to the left. Use the following key:

How well does the item you are reading
fit how you typically or generally feel?

1 = Fits Me Not at All
2 = Fits Me Slightly
3 = Fits Me Moderately
4 = Fits Me Very Well
5 = Fits Me Extremely Well

[INSERT ITEMS HERE]

—— 1. My heart beats fast, hard, or irregularly.
—— 2. My breathing feels hurried, shallow, or uneven.
—— 3. My muscles feel tight, tense, or clenched up (furrowed brow, making fist, clenching jaws, etc.).
—— 4. I feel restless and fidgety (tapping fingers or feet, fingering things, pacing, shifting in seat, chewing or biting, blinking, etc.).
—— 5. I feel tense or self-conscious when I say or do something.

— 6. I perspire too much or feel too warm.
— 7. I feel the need to go to the rest room even when I don't have to.
— 8. I feel uncoordinated.
— 9. My mouth feels dry.
— 10. I feel tired, fatigued, worn out, or exhausted.
— 11. I have a headache.
— 12. I feel unfit or heavy.
— 13. My back aches.
— 14. My shoulders, neck, or back feels tense.
— 15. The condition of my skin seems worse (too oily, blemishes).
— 16. My eyes are watering or teary.
— 17. My stomach is nervous and uncomfortable.
— 18. I have lost my appetite.

Note: This scale is an abbreviated version of Stress Inventory-6 (Smith, 1989; Smith & Seidel, 1982; Smith & Siebert, 1984). These items reflect four categories of physical stress symptoms as determined through factor analysis: basic physical stress symptoms (items 1–4), secondary physical stress symptoms (items 5–9), physical stress aftereffects (items 10–16), and digestive tract symptoms (items 17, 18). For more information see: Smith and Seidel, 1982 and Smith and Siebert, 1984.

In order to stimulate research on understudied dimensions of relaxation, permission is granted to reproduce this scale and all other scales introduced in this book for any noncommercial use. All other rights reserved.

1985; Tellegen & Atkinson, 1974), 16 PF Factors A and M (Carrington et al., 1980; Smith, 1978), openness to experience as assessed by the Fitzgerald Experience Inquiry (Fitzgerald, 1966; Lesh, 1970), and display low levels of intrusions or distractions in initial practice (Curtis, 1984). Additional questionnaires that have shown promise in relaxation research include the Focusing Inventory (Weinstein & Smith, 1989), the Phenomenology of Consciousness Inventory (Pekala & Levine, 1981), the profile of Trance, Imaging, and Meditation Experience (Brown, Forte, Rich, & Epstein, 1982), and the Profile of Meditation Experience (Maliszewski, Twemlow, Brown, & Angler, 1981). Finally, a list of words loosely suggestive of focusing, passivity, and receptivity can be assembled into provisional measures of relaxation skills (Table 3.4).

Each of these scales can be argued to partially measure relaxation skill. Absorption, frequently described in terms of focusing, is the ability to deploy "total attention . . . during which the available representational apparatus seems to be entirely dedicated to experiencing and modeling the attentional object, be it a landscape, a human being, a sound, a remembered incident, or an aspect of one's self" (Tellegen & Atkinson, 1974; p. 274). Additional Absorption Scale items may well tap passivity

TABLE 3.4 Provisional State and Trait Scales of Cognitive Dimensions of Relaxation

Below are the necessary components for constructing 10 scales (see table footnote). To assemble the desired scale (state or trait) combine the appropriate introduction with the desired group of items (somatic, focusing, passivity, receptivity and reinforcement). Delete all bracketed material. To score each scale simply add the item ratings.

[STATE INTRODUCTION]

The following items describe experiences people often have. Please carefully read each and indicate the extent to which it fits you *right now*, at the *present moment*. Rate all the items by putting numbers in the blanks to the left. Use the following key:

How well does the item you are reading fit
how you feel right now, at the present moment?

1 = Fits Me Not at All
2 = Fits Me Slightly
3 = Fits Me Moderately
4 = Fits Me Very Well
5 = Fits Me Extremely Well

[INSERT DESIRED GROUP OF ITEMS HERE]

[TRAIT INTRODUCTION]

The following items describe experiences people often have. Please read each carefully and indicate the extent to which it fits how you *typically or generally feel*. Rate all the items by putting numbers in the blanks to the left. Use the following key:

How well does the item you are reading
fit how you typically or generally feel?

1 = Fits Me Not at All
2 = Fits Me Slightly
3 = Fits Me Moderately
4 = Fits Me Very Well
5 = Fits Me Extremely Well

[INSERT DESIRED GROUP OF ITEMS HERE]

[SOMATIC ITEMS]

____ 1. Bathed	____ 11. High	____ 21. Sinking
____ 2. Caressed	____ 12. Light	____ 22. Slack
____ 3. Cool	____ 13. Limber	____ 23. Sleepy
____ 4. Dissolving	____ 14. Limp	____ 24. Slow
____ 5. Drowsy	____ 15. Liquid	____ 25. Smooth

[SOMATIC ITEMS] (continued)

___ 6. Elastic	___ 16. Loose	___ 26. Soft
___ 7. Flexible	___ 17. Massaged	___ 27. Supple
___ 8. Floating	___ 18. Mellow	___ 28. Throbbing
___ 9. Flowing	___ 19. Melting	___ 29. Tingling
___ 10. Heavy	___ 20. Sedate	___ 30. Warm

[FOCUSING ITEMS]

___ 1. Absorbed	___ 14. Conscious	___ 27. Mindful
___ 2. Alert	___ 15. Contemplative	___ 28. One-pointed
___ 3. At one	___ 16. Deep	___ 29. Pure
___ 4. Attentive	___ 17. Distant	___ 30. Quiet
___ 5. Awake	___ 18. Engrossed	___ 31. Radiant
___ 6. Aware	___ 19. Entranced	___ 32. Silent
___ 7. Bright	___ 20. Far Away	___ 33. Single-minded
___ 8. Captivated	___ 21. Fascinated	___ 34. Still
___ 9. Centered	___ 22. Focused	___ 35. Stimulated
___ 10. Charmed	___ 23. Glowing	___ 36. Transparent
___ 11. Cleansed	___ 24. Interested	___ 37. Undistracted
___ 12. Clear	___ 25. Lucid	
___ 13. Concentrated	___ 26. Meditative	

[PASSIVITY ITEMS]

___ 1. At ease	___ 13. Leisurely	___ 25. Selfless
___ 2. Carefree	___ 14. Letting be	___ 26. Settled
___ 3. Contented	___ 15. Letting go	___ 27. Simple
___ 4. Detached	___ 16. Listless	___ 28. Spontaneous
___ 5. Easy	___ 17. Motionless	___ 29. Surrendering
___ 6. Escaped	___ 18. Passive	___ 30. Unbothered
___ 7. Forgetting	___ 19. Patient	___ 31. Unencumbered
___ 8. Free	___ 20. Pausing	___ 32. Unforced
___ 9. Gentle	___ 21. Playful	___ 33. Unhurried
___ 10. Gratified	___ 22. Released	___ 34. Untroubled
___ 11. Indifferent	___ 23. Relieved	___ 35. Unworried
___ 12. Laid back	___ 24. Satisfied	

[RECEPTIVITY ITEMS]

___ 1. Accepting	___ 19. Immortal	___ 37. Rejuvenated
___ 2. Amazed	___ 20. Infinite	___ 38. Renewed
___ 3. Assured	___ 21. Innocent	___ 39. Reverent
___ 4. Awe	___ 22. Insightful	___ 40. Safe

TABLE 3.4 *(continued)*

[RECEPTIVITY ITEMS] *(continued)*

___ 5. Boundless	___ 23. Inspired	___ 41. Secure
___ 6. Childlike	___ 24. Intuitive	___ 42. Speechless
___ 7. Confident	___ 25. Liberated	___ 43. Spiritual
___ 8. Cosmic	___ 26. Loving	___ 44. Thankful
___ 9. Creative	___ 27. Mysterious	___ 45. Timeless
___ 10. Dreamy	___ 28. Mystical	___ 46. Touched
___ 11. Ecstatic	___ 29. New	___ 47. Transcendent
___ 12. Elated	___ 30. Open	___ 48. Transformed
___ 13. Encouraged	___ 31. Optimistic	___ 49. Trusting
___ 14. Enraptured	___ 32. Prayerful	___ 50. Unafraid
___ 15. Eternal	___ 33. Profound	___ 51. Wonder
___ 16. Expansive	___ 34. Reassured	___ 52. Wordless
___ 17. Glorious	___ 35. Reborn	___ 53. Worshipful
___ 18. Hopeful	___ 36. Receptive	

[REINFORCEMENT ITEMS]

___ 1. Able	___ 26. Energized	___ 51. Pleasured
___ 2. Actualized	___ 27. Enjoyable	___ 52. Poised
___ 3. Adjusted	___ 28. Even	___ 53. Positive
___ 4. Alive	___ 29. Exhilarated	___ 54. Recovered
___ 5. Answered	___ 30. Exultant	___ 55. Refreshed
___ 6. At home	___ 31. Fresh	___ 56. Relaxed
___ 7. Balanced	___ 32. Fun	___ 57. Rested
___ 8. Beautiful	___ 33. Good	___ 58. Restored
___ 9. Belonging	___ 34. Great	___ 59. Rewarded
___ 10. Blessed	___ 35. Happy	___ 60. Sensuous
___ 11. Blissful	___ 36. Harmonious	___ 61. Serene
___ 12. Calm	___ 37. Healing	___ 62. Soothed
___ 13. Capable	___ 38. Healthy	___ 63. Stable
___ 14. Cheerful	___ 39. In control	___ 64. Steady
___ 15. Collected	___ 40. Integrated	___ 65. Strengthened
___ 16. Comfortable	___ 41. In touch	___ 66. Strong
___ 17. Competent	___ 42. Invigorated	___ 67. Tranquil
___ 18. Complete	___ 43. Joyful	___ 68. Understanding
___ 19. Composed	___ 44. Knowing	___ 69. Unified
___ 20. Controlled	___ 45. Meaningful	___ 70. Uplifted
___ 21. Coordinated	___ 46. Natural	___ 71. Vigorous
___ 22. Coping	___ 47. Peaceful	___ 72. Vitalized
___ 23. Cozy	___ 48. Perceptive	___ 73. Whole
___ 24. Delighted	___ 49. Pleasant	___ 74. Wise
___ 25. Effective	___ 50. Pleased	___ 75. Wonderful

Note: This table provides all components needed to construct ten questionnaires: Relaxation Somatic Sensations Scale-State (RSSS-S), Relaxation Somatic Sensations Scale-Trait (RSSS-T), Focusing Scale-State (FS-S), Focusing Scale-Trait (FS-T), Passivity Scale-State (PS-S), Passivity Scale-Trait (PS-T), Receptivity Scale-State (RS-S), Receptivity Scale-Trait (RS-T), Relaxation Reinforcements Scale-State (RRS-S) and Relaxation Reinforcements Scale-Trait (RRS-T).

These items reflect solely the author's judgment of words associated with somatic relaxation, focusing, passivity, receptivity, and relaxation reinforcements. As such, they can be considered part of a provisional extended definition of these constructs. Statistical independence has yet to be determined. Because of the lack of reliability and validity research on these scales, use for other than research purposes is not advised. For advice on how to incorporate item groups in relaxation training, see Appendices B and C.

Focusing items primarily reflect:

1. *Deployment of attention toward a target stimulus.* (attentive, concentrated, fascinated, focused, interested, one-pointed, single-minded);

2. *Absence of distraction.* (cleansed, clear, distant, far away, pure, quiet, silent, still, transparent, undistracted);

3. *The degree to which a target stimulus is the sole object of attention, subjectively experienced as "absorbing."* (absorbed, at one, captivated, centered, charmed, contemplative, deep, engrossed, entranced, meditative, mindful); and

4. *The subjective experience of increased alertness which one might presume to contribute to increased attentiveness.* (alert, awake, aware, bright, conscious, glowing, lucid, radiant, stimulated).

Passivity items reflect:

1. *Reduced effort.* (at ease, easy, gentle, laid back, leisurely, listless, motionless, patient, settled, unforced, unhurried);

2. *The act of ceasing goal-directed or analytic activity.* (detached, forgetting, escaped, indifferent, letting be, letting go, passive, pausing, released, relieved, surrendering);

3. *Experienced contentment associated with reduced striving.* (contented, gratified, satisfied);

4. *Activity unencumbered by needless goal-directed or analytic striving* (carefree, free, playful, selfless, simple, spontaneous, unbothered, unencumbered, untroubled, unworried)

Receptivity items reflect:

1. *Positive experiences beyond the domain of what one appraises to be predictable, familiar, and easily understood.* (amazed, awe, boundless, cosmic, ecstatic, elated, enraptured, eternal, glorious, immortal, infinite, mysterious, mystical, new, prayerful, profound, reverent, speechless, spiritual, timeless, transcendent, wonder, wordless, worshipful);

2. *Openness to new experiences and insights.* (accepting, childlike, creative, dreamy, expansive, innocent, insightful, inspired, intuitive, loving, open, receptive);

3. *Experienced change or transformation.* (liberated, reborn, rejuvenated, renewed, touched, transformed); and

4. *Reduced level of experienced threat which one might presume to be associated with increased receptivity.* (assured, confident, encouraged, hopeful, optimistic, reassured, safe, secure, thankful, trusting, unafraid).

In addition, the following words describe the various reinforcing qualities of relaxation:

1. *General relaxation.* (calm, comfortable, peaceful, relaxed, rested, tranquil);

2. *Increased self-acceptance/harmony.* (adjusted, at home, balanced, belonging, col-

TABLE 3.4 *(continued)*

Note (continued):

   lected, complete, composed, even, harmonious, integrated, poised, stable, unified, whole);

   3. *Increased sense of health and well-being.* (alive, healing, healthy, invigorated, natural, recovered, restored);

   4. *Feelings of increased understanding (not necessarily associated with new insight).* (answered, in touch, knowing, meaningful, perceptive, understanding, wise);

   5. *Increased self-efficacy.* (able, actualized, capable, competent, controlled, coordinated, coping, effective, energized, in control, steady, strengthened, strong, vigorous, vitalized); and

   6. *General positive states.* (beautiful, blessed, blissful, cheerful, cozy, delighted, enjoyable, exhilarated, exultant, fresh, fun, good, great, happy, joyful, pleasant, pleased, pleasured, positive, refreshed, rewarded, sensuous, serene, soothed, uplifted, wonderful).

("Sometimes thoughts and images come to me without the slightest effort on my part.") and receptivity ("I sometimes 'step outside' my usually self and experience an entirely different state of being.").

Sixteen PF Factor A, *sizothymia* might appear to reflect one aspect of focusing, a "blocking of easy interaction with the changing external world" as well as receptive beliefs, values, and commitments reflecting "a high level of interest in symbolic and subjective activity" (Cattell, 1957). Similarly, 16 PF Factor M, *autia*, seems related to focusing, passivity, as well as receptivity. *Autic* individuals have interests in "art, theory, basic beliefs, and spiritual matters." They can "dissociate" and engage in "autonomous, self-absorbed relaxation" enabling them to be "imaginatively enthralled by inner creations," "charmed by works of the imagination," and "completely absorbed" in the momentum of their own thoughts, following them "wherever they lead, for their intrinsic attractiveness and with neglect of realistic considerations" (Cattell, 1957).

A few relatively unused instruments also deserve mention. The Fitzgerald (1966) Experience Inquiry, appears to be a receptivity measure tapping the tendency not to be "bound by the conventional modes of thought, memory, and perception." The Van Nuys (1973) intrusion count is a simple subjective report (by means of a hand-counter) of the number of distractions one experiences in relaxation. As such, it is a fairly direct measure of focusing and possibly passivity (letting go of distraction). The Focusing Inventory (Weinstein & Smith, 1988, Smith, 1989), consist of items rated by "experts" as depicting focusing. The

Profile of Meditation Experience (Maliszewski, Twemlow, Brown, & Angler, 1981), profile of Trance, Imaging, and Meditation Experience (Brown, Forte, Rich, & Epstein, 1982), and Phenomenology of Consciousness Inventory (Pekala & Levine, 1981) tap a broad range of experiences possibly reflecting all three dimensions of focusing, passivity, and receptivity. Finally, Table 3.4 lists terms I have found useful when defining focusing, passivity, and receptivity to relaxation students and clients.

Taken together, at least 12 instruments are available as provisional operationalizations of the skills central to our cognitive-behavioral model. Table 3.5 compares the relative emphasis of each. It is unfortunate that relaxation researchers have tended to ignore tools that may well have considerable potential for deepening our understanding of relaxation.

So far, we have considered arousal and skill-based criteria for depth of relaxation. As we have seen, the cognitive-behavioral model predicts that reductions in arousal and increments in focusing, passivity, and receptivity can be rewarding. If so, then the emergence of generally-

TABLE 3.5 Operationalizations of Focusing, Passivity, and Receptivity

Scale	Focusing	Passivity	Receptivity
	Dimension Tapped		
Tellegen Absorption Scale*	X	X	X
16 PF—Sizothymia	X		X
16 PF—Autia	X	X	X
Fitzgerald Experience Inquiry			X
Van Nuys Intrusion Count	X	X	
Focusing Inventory	X		
Profile of Meditation Experience	X	X	X
Profile of Trance, Imaging, and Meditation	X	X	X
Phenomenology of Consciousness Inventory	X	X	X
Focusing Trait/State Scale	X		
Passivity Trait/State Scale		X	
Receptivity Trait/State Scale			X

*Tellegen Absorption Scale (Tellegen & Atkinson, 1974); The 16 Personality Factor Questionnaire (Cattell, Eber, & Tatsouka, 1970); the Fitzgerald Experience Inquiry (Fitzgerald, 1966); the Van Nuys Intrusion Count (Van Nuys, 1973); the Focusing Inventory (Weinstein & Smith, 1989); the Profile of Meditation Experience (Maliszewski et al., 1981); Profile of Trance, Imaging, and Meditation Experience (Brown et al., 1982); and Phenomenology of Consciousness Inventory (Pekala & Levine, 1981). The Focusing, Passivity, and Receptivity Trait/State Scales are presented in Table 3.4.

rewarding appraisals of relaxation can be a sign of depth. A partial catalog of terms depicting potentially rewarding relaxation states is presented in Table 3.4.

THE SEARCH FOR STRUCTURAL CRITERIA OF DEPTH

In Chapter 2 I suggested that, as relaxation progresses, increasingly abstract and differentiated relaxation structures are acquired. If so, the degree of abstraction and differentiation of reported within-session relaxation experiences can serve as indicators of depth. To elaborate, a relaxer who reports, "I felt I was letting go of needless control" is describing an experience more abstract than, "I felt I was letting go of shoulder muscle tension." However, if this person is unable to differentiate the concrete applications and implications of "letting go," the phrase is little more than a slogan or platitude and the experienced level of relaxation is still relatively shallow. In contrast, if our relaxer has a richly differentiated understanding of letting go ("In my experience, letting go means not worrying needlessly about the future, delegating authority at work, trusting that things will work out even if I don't plan them, surrendering cherished but unrealistic goals, etc"), then we have an indication that a deeper level of relaxation has been achieved.

Taken alone, abstraction and differentiation have limited value as criteria for assessing relaxation. It would be more useful to know the content and function of structures associated with depth. An assessment could then proceed to look for specific structures that serve the relaxer in specific ways. To my knowledge, there is no assessment tool that accomplishes this. However, frequent references to deep relaxation can be found in studies on hypnosis, meditation, and altered states of consciousness. It is worth examining this literature for possible structure-based operationalizations of depth of relaxation.

Hypnosis

The concept of hypnotic depth and susceptibility has been clearly operationalized. Standardized tests typically include a series of suggested tasks of progressive difficulty. The more tasks one "passes," the more deeply one is hypnotized. The Stanford, Harvard, and Barber scales (Barber & Wilson, 1978/1979; Shor & Orne, 1962; Weitzenhoffer & Hilgard, 1962) are among the most widely applied, and include items

TABLE 3.6 Content of Scales of Hypnotic Depth and Susceptibility*

Postural sway (responding to suggestions to fall backwards)
Head falling
Eye closure
Hand lowering (responding to suggestions that one cannot resist lowering hand)
Arm immobilization (cannot move arm)
Finger lock (cannot open fingers)
Arm rigidity (cannot bend arm)
Moving hands (cannot resist moving hands together or apart)
Verbal inhibition (cannot say name or home town when asked)
Communication inhibition (cannot talk at all)
Hallucination (sees fly or mosquito that is not there)
Eye catalepsy (cannot open closed eyes)
Posthypnotic suggestion (suggestion to change chairs after end of session)
Posthypnotic amnesia (suggestion to forget up to 3 items presented in session)
Taste hallucination (sweet-sour)
Dream
Age regression (to 5th or 2nd grades)
Anosmia (loss of sense of smell when tested with ammonia)
Hallucination (voice)
Visual hallucination (boxes)

*Barber & Wilson, 1978/1979; Shor & Orne, 1962; Weitzenhoffer & Hilgard, 1962

ranging from suggested postural sway and head falling, to hallucinations, posthypnotic suggestion, and age regression (Table 3.6).

Hypnotic depth can also be defined subjectively in terms of one's perception or recollection of what has transpired during a session. Although there is some debate as to what (if any) experiences constitute a "hypnotic state," Hilgard and Hilgard (1975) have suggested:

> Sense of Relaxation: Subject experiences vary. A typical report might include "It is a relaxation such as I have never experienced before: very deep, complete, with escape from all tension."

> Narrowing of Attention: The mind may seem "almost blank, attending scarcely at all." Or attention may be only on the hypnotist's voice or suggestions, inattentive to distractions. "It's like narrowing the thread of existence to a single strand, so that things that usually matter seem to drop away one by one. All that is left is the hypnotist and the hypnotist's voice." Such narrowing can represent a fading of "reality orientation," or awareness of the future or past so that one experiences a timeless, carefree state.

> Imaginative Involvement: Hallucinations or age regression can have a "day-dream quality," or be as vividly real as an actual dream.

Awareness of Suggestibility: Contrary to popular opinion, hypnotic subjects are often aware of their heightened suggestibility. In most cases, the subject is aware of retaining an element of control, and realize they can resist suggestions if they so desire.

Finally, hypnotic depth has been rated by means of a simple subjective number scale. A subject may be told that "0 is for feeling wide awake, 1, drifting into a drowsy state, 2, beginning to feel hypnotized, 3, feeling that hypnosis has been entered," and so on. During hypnosis, a subject can be instructed to move from level to level, simply by suggesting a number. Interesting effects have been claimed for open-ended scales (Tart, 1967, 1970). First, traditional responsiveness appears not to require depths beyond 8 or 10 for most subjects. Second, at great depths (up to 100), responsiveness to suggestions appears to cease spontaneously and even communication with the hypnotist may become essentially absent. Subjective reports at such levels vary, and have been described as "mystical," including loss of awareness of or identification with one's body, restricted or narrowing of awareness of the environment, perception of a slowing and eventually stopping of time, and an eventual cessation of all spontaneous mental activity. However, such reports must be viewed with considerable caution since they have not been widely replicated. Furthermore, since they are essentially individual responses to the ambiguous suggestion "depth," they may be colored heavily by individual philosophical or religious assumptions as to what constitutes a "deep experience."

The applicability of criteria for hypnotic depth to relaxation depends on where hypnotically-induced relaxation fits in our cognitive-behavioral model. First, the fact that many hypnosis protocols rely heavily on autogenic and imagery suggestions suggests that hypnotic relaxation falls in the same class as these approaches ("unrestrictive" approaches as described in Chapter 4). In addition, intermediate levels of passivity may be required for hypnotic responsivity. One may well need to be sufficiently passive to cease interfering goal-directed and analytic striving, but still active enough respond to suggestions from an appraised external source. Progressive relaxation, stretching, and breathing exercises may be too active for this to happen. In contemplation, meditation, and "deep" hypnosis responding to any suggestion may represent a distracting excess of activity. Finally, hypnotic responsivity may be associated with the acquisition of a specific set of cognitive structures, for example a belief that one can be hypnotized, a valuing of the potential benefits of hypnosis, and a commitment to put aside skepticism and "go along" with hypnotist instructions.

However, it may be a mistake to assume that hypnotic responsivity is a defining characteristic of any level of relaxation. Few experts equate hypnosis with relaxation; indeed, subjects can be highly anxious or aroused (and even ride an exercycle) while being hypnotized (Hilgard, 1977). In addition, it is tempting to speculate that levels of passivity associated with hypnosis may, in different contexts, form the basis for quite different phenomena. A religiously inclined individual may report a particularly meaningful experience of prayer or communion with God; a Zen meditator may encounter vivid hallucinatory distractions; and a patient in psychoanalysis, strongly emotional recollections of childhood conflicts. In other words, when intermediate levels of passivity are reached, the content of experience may be a function of one's cognitive structures, that is, how one construes the situation, or what one appraises to be the external source of influence (i.e., "responding to the suggestions of a hypnotist while in a hypnotic trance," "communing with God," " facing illusion," or "uncovering unconscious conflict").

In terms of cognitive-behavioral theory, hypnosis is not a global system of relaxation, but just one approach among many. Given the ambiguities concerning the nature of hypnosis and its relationship to relaxation, it is risky to rely on this area of study for criteria of depth of relaxation. More seriously, popular conceptualizations of hypnosis rely heavily on descriptions of states rather than cognitive structures. Perhaps a related area of research, meditation, can provide us with a more useful set of assessment strategies.

Meditation

An enormous literature has examined the concept of depth in meditation from a philosophical and religious perspective. In addition, a number of ambitious attempts have been made to integrate psychological and spiritual concepts of development (Wilber, Engler, & Brown, 1986). However one instrument used in two early studies (Maupin, 1965; Lesh, 1970), is worth noting. After reviewing the literature on Zen, Maupin developed a rating scale that identifies five levels of meditative experience:

> Type A: Dizziness and fogginess. This initial level is characterized by a feelings of "dizziness," "befogged consciousness," "feeling like going under an anesthetic or being hypnotized." Often the experience is somewhat unpleasant.

Type B: Relaxation and calmness. One feels increased degrees of calm and relaxation. However, concentration need not be sustained.

Type C: Pleasant body sensations. One may feel a variety of pleasant body sensations, such as "vibrations," "waves," or feeling as though the body is "suspended" or "light." Concentration is more sustained.

Type D: Vivid breathing sensations. Breathing is experienced as "vivid" and sustained. Belly movements may seem larger, or one may feel "filled with air." Concentration seems almost effortless.

Type E: Concentration and detachment. The deepest level of meditation is characterized by a "very lucid state of consciousness which is deeply satisfying." There is a "nonstriving" attitude, and one is able to take a calmly detached view of any thoughts and feelings which might happen to emerge. Concentration seems to be easy and fairly complete. This level is frequently accompanied by extensive loss of body feelings.

Subsequent researchers have had little success agreeing upon what constitutes a "deep" meditative experience (Pekala, 1987). Descriptions have been truly diverse, and have included: "feeling of merging with others," "oneness with the external," "elation" (Osis, Bokert, & Carlson, 1973; Kohr, 1984), transcending the "limitations of three-dimensional reality," letting go of "negative emotion," (Kohr, 1984), and decreased somatic arousal and internal dialogue (Pekala, Wenger, & Levine, 1985). However, even if a consensus were to emerge on the characteristics of a "deep" meditative state, it would have limited value for us. Once again, our main interest is in finding ways of defining depth in terms of structures rather than states.

Altered States of Consciousness

Perhaps the two most widely cited researchers of altered states of consciousness (ASCs) are Charles Tart and Abraham Maslow. Their definitions would appear to offer some promise for our search for structural criteria for depth of relaxation. Tart (1975) has defined an ASC as a "unique, dynamic pattern of configuration of psychological structures, an active system of psychological substructures." For Maslow (1971) one important type of ASC is the "peak experience," a momentarily intense state reflecting "Being-values" (values associated with self-actualization).

Even though these ASC definitions make note of structures, research has focused almost exclusively on cataloging ASC states (Tart, 1969; 1975; Zinberg, 1977). However, investigators have provided us with an unexpected key to understanding depth of relaxation in structural terms. Examine how Tart and Maslow have considered relaxation at a personal and practical level. Tart has presented a system for enhancing "self-awareness" based on the Russian mystic and philosopher Gurdjieff (Tart, 1987). Criteria for depth are defined in terms of the level of consciousness one achieves, ranging from "ordinary sleeping and dreaming" and "consensus trance" to "genuine self-consciousness" and "objective consciousness." Maslow (1971), somewhat less systematically, has recommended attending and listening to the world "in a very specific way which can be called Taoistic—silently, hushed, quietly, fully listening, noninterfering, receptive, patient, respectful of the matter-in-hand, courteous to the matter-in-hand." (p. 120)

My point is not that the thinking of Gurdjieff or Taoism provide useful tools for understanding relaxation; these systems work for some and not for others. More important is that Tart and Maslow both required the assistance of a special type of structure, an encompassing philosophical or religious point of view when attempting to apply their notions to everyday life. This is not a coincidence, but a preference of many researchers of relaxation and states of consciousness. Such encompassing structures, and not the attributes of an ASC or peak experience, point to a strategy for assessing deeper levels of relaxation. As we shall see, it is a strategy that can go beyond examining the degree of abstraction and differentiation of relaxation structures.

THE PATH AND PARADOX OF RELAXATION

I have proposed that relaxation deepens and generalizes because of the operation of skill mastery and cognitive restructuring cycles. However, from relaxer's perspective, the most salient feature of this global process is the *paradox of passivity*. In many of life's endeavors, success results from goal-directed and analytic striving; yet in relaxation, growth and movement occur in the absence of such activity.

There are two aspects of this paradox worth noting. First, the less one tries to control or direct an exercise, the better it works. In progressive relaxation one must let go in order to experience any relaxation effect; holding on will render the exercise useless. Yoga stretching and breathing exercises simply cannot be completed with strain and effort. "Passive volition," that is, trying without trying, is central to effective autogenic training and imagery. And striving for success in meditation simply creates needless distraction. In all relaxation, movement paradoxically occurs when one ceases goal-directed activity.

Furthermore, such movement may have a direction of its own, one not constructed through the relaxer's analytic efforts. To elaborate, we have seen that each act of focusing, passivity, and receptivity can automatically contribute to the deepening of relaxation through the operation of the skill mastery cycle. A relaxer may be quite unaware of the implications of his actions, that is, the chain of potential changes he is capable of setting into motion. Similarly, each supporting structure may imply additional structures outside the awareness of the relaxer. A person committed to letting go of tension in the relaxation session may soon discover this commitment implies letting go of irrational and distressing thoughts as well. This committment may in turn imply other commitments, such as letting go of the desire to control all things at work, surrendering cherished attachments, accepting life's joys and misfortunes, and so on. In sum, the universe of relaxation experiences is not random, but is structured by an underlying fabric of implications. Relaxation has the potential for movement and direction that exists outside of the deliberate efforts of the relaxer.

A *transcendent metaphor* is a special structure that enables the relaxer to understand the course of relaxation in terms of this paradox. Such a metaphor defines the direction relaxation can take and provides criteria for depth. Consider, for example, the metaphor of the path.

A path exists outside of the deliberate goal-directed and analytic striving of the traveller. It provides direction, signposts, and distance markers, although the end point may not be seen or known. The traveller is not entirely passive, but must deploy certain skills in order to progress. Finally, the traveller, in order to move, must have certain beliefs, values, and commitments with regard to the path, for example, that it is worth travelling, it does have direction. The idea of path and traveler can serve as a neutral metaphor (one that makes no metaphysical assumptions) of the overall nature and course of relaxation.

Relaxation traditions provide us with a rich variety of alternative, often considerably less neutral, transcendent metaphors. We have seen that Tart and Maslow have chosen those of Gurdjieff and Taoism. Others metaphors exist, and it can be useful to put our own preferences and biases aside and note them with an open mind:

> Relaxation can be a way of nurturing internal healing processes; depth is the experience of health and well-being.
>
> Relaxation can be clearing the windows of perception; depth is clarity of vision.
>
> Relaxation can be a road to enlightenment, a way of dissolving the bonds of ego, attachment, and illusion; depth is freedom and spontaneity.

Relaxation can be way of accessing the internal creative resources; depth is insight.

Relaxation can be a royal road to the unconscious; depth is the release of repressed impulse.

And relaxation can be prayer, a way of coming into harmony with God's will; depth is the experience of grace.

In terms of cognitive-behavioral relaxation training, such metaphors provide a context for understanding a variety of relaxation experiences. Each is consistent with the paradox of passivity and recognizes that movement can occur and have direction even when goal-directed and analytic activity have been put aside. From the relaxer's perspective, such metaphors point to processes perceived to operate beyond, or transcend, one's efforts or understanding.

When a client articulates a useful and meaningful transcendent metaphor, he or she puts a living face on relaxation processes and defines a path that can be subjectively real, important, and worth traveling. Furthermore, such metaphors can facilitate the deployment of relaxation skills. Target stimuli acquire increased salience, contributing to motivation to maintain attentional focus ("I take seriously the task of attending to my meditation stimulus because I believe meditative processes can help me see the world more clearly"). The belief that relaxation processes can operate outside deliberate goal-directed and analytic activity permits enhanced passivity ("I believe my unconscious can and will offer me creative insights if I put aside efforts to solve my problems all on my own"). Finally, a transcendent metaphor offers justification for the hope that relaxation will yield unseen rewards, a reason for maintaining a stance of receptivity ("God has a hidden plan for my life; in the silence of my contemplation I can trust that God is at work").

Transcendent metaphors provide the relaxer with a new vocabulary for describing focusing, passivity, and receptivity. For example, the relaxer who sincerely believes that the course of relaxation is guided by internal healing processes, the creative unconscious, God, or unnamed sources beyond immediate and deliberate detection or control, may describe acts of focusing, passivity, or receptivity as "absorption," "detachment," "surrender," "humility," "letting be," or "reverence."

Similarly, a transcendent metaphor can provide a new vocabulary for describing convergent and divergent activity. For example, a client may have decided that the essence of relaxation is to "clear the windows of perception in order to view things objectively." This metaphor permits us to see a difficult practice session, one with considerable divergent activity, as "clouded with illusion and distraction." In contrast, a convergent session may be experienced as "clear and vivid." To take another example, a client may experience relaxation as prayer. Convergent and divergent activity may be seen as representing phases of "communion" or perceived "distance from God."

It should be clear that transcendent metaphors can serve many functions. Most important, they organize a wide range of relaxation processes, facilitate the recall and application a variety of subordinate beliefs, values, and commitments, and, as a result, economize the task of mastering relaxation. However, it should be noted that such metaphors differ in level of generality. Those of *limited domain* apply primarily to the relaxation session (relaxation as a way of nurturing internal healing processes, of accessing the "unconscious," etc.), while those of *open domain* can also apply to life at large (relaxation as a way of clearing the windows of perception, a road to enlightenment, a form of prayer, etc).

In conclusion, a structural assessment of depth of relaxation must first determine if a client has articulated a differentiated, transcendent metaphor. If present, such a metaphor can provide its own definition of what happens in relaxation and criteria for depth. However, there are serious risks in assessing depth of relaxation in terms of transcendent metaphors supplied by clients. Such assessments supplement, but do not replace, appraisals of arousal reduction and skill mastery. Furthermore, a therapist must carefully avoid imposing any personally preferred metaphor on a client. It is all too easy to be a magician or priest, promoting a private vision of internal healing potentials, enlightenment, the unconscious, God, and so on. A more useful role is that of a neutral guide, respecting whatever path is real for the client and alert to paths that may be counterproductive.

CHAPTER 4

The Relaxation Hierarchy

The cognitive-behavoral model we have presented offers a new way of understanding the process of relaxation. Perhaps one of the most profound implications of this model is that different relaxation procedures are not interchangeable, but work in different ways for different people. Strong evidence for this can be found in the preference of traditional schools of relaxation for exercise combinations (see Appendix A for a complete description of traditional relaxation). If all approaches to relaxation are interchangeable, there should be no need to include more than one exercise.

More important, most major schools of relaxation display consistencies in the order exercises are taught (Table 4.1). For example, progressive relaxation is often taught before breathing (Benson, 1975) and simple somatic autogenic exercises (Bernstein & Borkovec, 1973; Edmonston, 1986); yoga stretching before breathing (Rama, Ballentine, & Ajaya, 1976); breathing before meditation (Rama, Ballentine, & Ajaya, 1976; Benson, 1975); simple autogenic exercises before imagery (Luthe, 1969-1973) and meditation (Kapleau, 1965), and so on.

Although no system incorporates all types of relaxation, there is sufficient overlap to enable us to piece together a composite "cross-sectional" sequence, a relaxation hierarchy of nine modalities of approaches (Appendix A):

1. Progressive relaxation
2. Hatha yoga stretching

TABLE 4.1 Comparison of exercise sequences for major approaches to relaxation

Component In Sequence	Relaxation Approaches*					
	Traditional Yoga	Zen Meditation	Autogenic Training	Progressive Relaxation	Traditional Hypnosis	Benson's Method
Progressive Relaxation				1	1	1
Yoga Stretching (Hatha)	1					
Breathing	2					2
Autogenic "warmth/heaviness"; sensations of relaxation in skeletal muscles; relaxation by recall			1	2	2	
Autogenic internal focus (abdomen, heart, etc.)			2			
Imagery (Simple stimuli)			3		3	
Imagery ("Unconscious answers")			4			
Concentrative meditation (counting breaths, mantra, etc.)	3	2				3
Zen/Mindfulness Meditation ("Just sitting"; openness to flow of all stimuli)		3				

*Traditional yoga (Iyengar, 1965; Rama et al., 1976); Zen (Kapleau, 1965); autogenic training (Luthe, 1969–1973); progressive relaxation (Bernstein & Borkovec, 1973); traditional hypnosis (Edmonston, 1986); Benson's method (1975; 1984)

Note: See Appendix A for detailed description of approaches.

3. Breathing; Lamaze; pranayama
4. Initial autogenic and hypnosis warmth-heaviness formulae; attending to muscle sensations associated with relaxation; relaxation by recall
5. Autogenic/Zen internal organ formulae, kundalini yoga
6. Beginning autogenic/hypnosis imagery (simple forms, everyday objects, scenes)
7. Advanced autogenic/hypnotic imagery ("inner adviser," "answers from the unconscious" techniques); various creativity exercises; Gendlin's "focusing"
8. Concentrative meditation (Benson's method, clinically standardized meditation; Zen breath counting, TM)
9. Zen "just sitting"

This hierarchy is not a coincidence, but is partially repeated again and again around the world wherever combinations of relaxation exercises are taught. However, since exercises tend to be presented as blends, it can be difficult to understand the reason underlying the relaxation hierarchy. Elsewhere, I have offered unconfounded or "pure" versions of approaches on our hierarchy (Smith, 1986a, 1986b, 1987, 1989). By examining the form and content of instructions prototypical or representative of each level, we can see a pattern in terms of the four dimensions of our cognitive-behavioral model, focusing, passivity, receptivity, and structure abstraction/differentiation. First, relaxation exercises appear to be either physical or mental. In addition, mental exercises can be divided according to those that incorporate an unrestricted or restricted focal task; autogenic and imagery tasks permit considerable leeway in how one attends to "warmth and "heaviness" or fantasy images, whereas meditative approaches prescribe a highly restricted focal stimulus. As we shall see, the closer we look, the more a pattern emerges. (See Table 4.2 for a complete list of exercises for each level of the hierarchy.)

PHYSICAL APPROACHES

Isometric Squeeze Relaxation

The most widely used approach to relaxation in North America is variously called progressive relaxation, Jacobsonian relaxation, and deep muscle relaxation (Appendix A). Although frequently this approach blends relaxation strategies (most often breathing, imagery,

TABLE 4.2 Exercise examples for each level of the relaxation hierarchy

Physical Exercises

Isometric Squeeze Relaxation

Hand Squeeze ("Make a fist . . . let go")
Arm Squeeze ("Tighten arm at elbow . . .")
Arm and Side Squeeze ("Press arm to your side . . .")
Back Squeeze ("Tighten up your lower back . . .")
Shoulder Squeeze ("Shrug your shoulders . . .")
Back of Neck Squeeze ("Tilt your head back, squeezing the back of your neck . . .")
Face Squeeze ("Squeeze all your face muscles . . .")
Front of Neck Squeeze ("Tilt your head forward, squeezing the front of your neck . . .")
Stomach and Chest Squeeze ("Squeeze your stomach and chest . . .")
Leg Squeeze ("Pull your leg in towards your body and squeeze . . .")
Foot Squeeze ("Push your toes into the ground and squeeze . . .")

Yogaform Stretching

Hand Stretch ("Open your fingers and stretch . . .")
Arm Stretch ("Reach your arm out in front of you . . .")
Arm and Side Stretch ("Stretch your arm high in the air . . .")
Back Stretch ("Bow over, stretching your back . . .")
Shoulder Stretch ("Cross your arms in front of you, stretching your shoulders . . .")
Back of Neck Stretch ("Let your head hang forward, stretching the back of your neck . . .")
Face Stretch ("Open your jaws, mouth, and eyes . . .")
Front of Neck Stretch ("Let your head hang back, stretching the front of your neck . . .")
Stomach and Chest Stretch ("Lean back and stretch your stomach and chest out . . .")
Leg Stretch ("Stretch your leg out in front of you . . .")
Foot Stretch ("Pull your toes up towards your head . . .")

Breathing Relaxation

Deep Breathing ("Slowly take a deep breath and exhale . . .")
Arm Swing Breathing ("Cross your arms in front of you while exhaling . . .")
Breathing and Bowing ("Bow forward while breathing out . . .")
Breathing and Stretching ("Reach to the sky while breathing in, bow forward while breathing out . . .")
Stomach Squeeze Breathing ("Squeeze your stomach with your hands while exhaling . . .")
Active Diaphragmatic Breathing ("Pull your stomach in towards your back while exhaling . . .")
Inhaling Through Nose ("Slowly inhale through your nose . . .")
Exhaling Through Lips ("Slowly exhale through your opened lips . . .")
Focused Breathing ("Quietly attend to the flow of breath . . .")

Unrestrictive Mental Exercises

Somatic Focusing-I

Mental Isometric Relaxation ("Attend to a muscle group and let go of tension . . .")
Mental Massage ("Imagine fingers massaging your back . . .")
Warmth and Heaviness ("Think 'warm and heavy' . . .")

Somatic Focusing-II

Abdomen ("Imagine soothing warmth in your abdomen . . .")
Erect Spine ("Imagine energy flowing up your erect spine . . .")
Heart ("Let your heart beat slowly and evenly . . .")
Base of Throat ("Let your throat open and relax . . .")
Visual Phenomena ("Attend to darkness you see with your eyes closed . . .")

Thematic Imagery

Pleasure ("Imagine you are preparing your favorite meal . . .")
Escape ("Escape to a private island . . .")
Reminiscence ("Think of your childhood home . . .")
Mastery ("Imagine the good feelings of success at mastering a challenge . . .")
Intuition ("Ask your 'inner guide' a question and wait for a response . . .")
Sensation ("Attend to the wind and sun against your skin . . .")

Restrictive Mental Exercises

Contemplation

Contemplation on Personal Strengths ("Quietly attend to your good points . . .")
Contemplation on Relaxation ("Attend to the crux or gist of what it means to feel relaxed . . .")

Centered Focus Meditation

Rocking Meditation ("Gently rock back and forth, as if you were in a boat . . .")
Counting Breaths ("With every outgoing breath, count 'one' . . .")
Relaxing Word or Phrase ("Quietly let a relaxing word or phrase repeat in your mind . . .")
Neutral Syllable (Mantra) ("Quietly let a neutral syllable repeat in your mind . . .")
Visual Image ("In your mind's eye, picture a simple visual image . . .")
External Stimulus ("With your eyes half open, attend to a simple external stimulus . . .")

Open Focus Meditation

Attending to Sounds ("Listen to the sounds around you as they come and go . . . do not dwell on any one sound . . .")
Attending to Visual Images ("Attend to whatever mental images come and go . . . do not dwell on any specific image . . .")
Attending to the Flow of all Stimuli ("Attend to all stimuli as they come and go . . . do not dwell on any stimulus . . .")

(Smith, 1987, 1989)

and occasionally stretching), its central feature is actively creating and releasing muscle tension. For this reason, such exercises can be generically termed *isometric squeeze relaxation* (Smith, 1989). It is a familiar approach, incorporating isometric motions one may well display in everyday life (making a fist, shrugging, grimacing, etc.) In addition, initial exercises call for relatively little focusing since the act of clenching in itself generates an easily detected "relaxation rebound," and attention is directed to a variety of stimuli by continuous patter from the instructor. The following segment illustrates the key components of isometric squeeze relaxation (Smith, 1989, p.75):

> Move your attention up to your neck and gently tilt your head back. While keeping the rest of your body relaxed, gently press the back of your head against your neck *now*.
> Let the tension grow, this time not too tightly.
> Create a good, complete squeeze.
> And *let go*.
> [PAUSE]
> Let the muscles of your neck relax like a floppy rag doll.
> Let the tension unwind.
> Enjoy the feelings of relaxation.
> Let the momentum of relaxation carry the tension away.

Yogaform Stretching

There are many forms of yoga and most blend relaxation techniques with religious teachings and behavioral restrictions (Appendix A). However, the simplest forms of yoga place central importance on slowly, smoothly, and gently stretching various muscle groups. We can generically term such an approach (to distinguish it from yoga philosophy and religion) *yogaform stretching*. Compared with squeezing, stretching is more focused, passive, and possibly receptive, as can be seen in the following prototypical exercise (Smith, 1989, pp. 100–101):

> Now, while sitting erect, let your head tilt easily toward your chest.
> [PAUSE]
> Try not to force it down.
> [PAUSE]
> Simply let gravity pull your head down.
> [PAUSE]

Farther and farther.

[PAUSE]

Feel the stretch in the back of your neck.

[PAUSE]

As the force of gravity easily and slowly pulls your head down.

[PAUSE]

When you are ready

[PAUSE]

Gently and easily lift your head.

[PAUSE]

Lift it until it is again comfortably upright.

This neck stretch is considerably more focused and passive than the preceding neck squeeze. First, it incorporates more pauses and less attention-directing patter. There is more "silent time" in which one might become distracted. Also, the movement suggested, tilting the head forward, is intrinsically passive—one simply relaxes and lets gravity pull the weight of the head down on its own. One actually does very little, whereas in the corresponding neck squeeze, one begins by actively tensing up and letting go. (It should be noted that other stretches, such as extending the arms, are somewhat less passive. Even in these exercises, the major muscle group, here the biceps, is "stretched," while the minor muscle group, the triceps, actually does the work.) Finally, one can speculate that fewer activities in life involve slowly, smoothly, and gently stretching in contrast to rapidly and effortfully squeezing. Stretching, as described here, is perhaps to many a somewhat less familiar activity, one requiring a bit more receptivity.

Breathing

The goal of many breathing exercises is to increase the involvement of the diaphragm and foster a rhythmical breathing pattern (Appendix A). Often physical stretches or imagery are utilized to achieve this goal. However, a prototypical breathing exercise involves simply attending to the flow of breath (Smith, 1989, p. 128):

Now continue breathing in a relaxed manner, in and out through your nose.

[PAUSE 5 SECONDS]

Try not to force your breathing.

[PAUSE 5 SECONDS]

Notice the air as it rushes in and out, flowing into and out of your lungs, filling your body with refreshing and relaxing air.

[PAUSE 5 SECONDS]

Notice the unhurried rhythm of your breathing. Let yourself breathe effortlessly, without strain.

[PAUSE 10 SECONDS]

This segment takes just as much time as the preceding isometric squeeze and stretch exercises. However, the pauses are longer and their are fewer words, placing an increased demanding on focusing skill. Focusing is made even more difficult by the absence of a single, discernable concrete stimulus; the flow of breath, past the nostrils, down breathing passages, and into the lungs, is not an easy target of attention. In addition, the process of breathing is one of the few physiological functions that is both active and passive since breathing can continue on its own with no overt effort. Finally, since relatively few everyday activities call for simple attending to breath, breathing exercises may well be intrinsically less familiar, and more demanding of receptivity, than either stretching or isometric squeeze relaxation.

UNRESTRICTIVE MENTAL EXERCISES

Somatic Focusing: Level I

Initial autogenic and hypnosis exercises incorporate phrases that direct attention to somatic sensations related to relaxation (Appendix A). For example:

Simply let thoughts related to warmth and heaviness float through your mind, like echoes.

[PAUSE 10 SECONDS]

Think the phrase "My hands and arms are heavy and warm . . . warmth is flowing into my hands and arms."

[PAUSE]

What pictures or images come to mind that go with warmth and heaviness? You might want to imagine your hands and arms in warm, soothing water, or in the sand. You might want to imagine a warm, relaxing breeze caressing your skin. Let pictures and images come to mind that suggest warmth and heaviness. (Smith, 1989, p. 144)

Such exercises illustrate initial levels of *somatic focusing*. They have a number of features in common. First, attention is directed to physical signs of relaxation manifested in the skin and skeletal muscles. Also, these exercises are relatively unrestrictive concerning the content of imagery. As long as one thinks "warm and heavy," a wide range of images and associated phrases are permitted.

Such somatic focusing may or may not require any more focusing or receptivity than any of the preceding approaches. However, it clearly requires more passivity since no physical movement is involved. In addition, considerable emphasis is placed on not actively attempting to generate sensations, but passively and indifferently letting words and thoughts pass by.

Somatic Focusing, Level II

Advanced autogenic, kundalini yoga, and some Zen exercises shift the focus of attention from relatively external musculature and skin to deep internal processes, organs, and nerve centers, including the abdomen, heart, throat, spine, and so on (Appendix A). Once again, the goal is to attend to phrases or sensations associated with physiological relaxation. Here is an exercise involving the heart:

> Now let warm and pleasant relaxation flow up to your chest, around your heart.
>
> [PAUSE 10 SECONDS]
>
> Let warmth flow, like a calm river, or the moving rays of the sun, up to the area of your heart, deep within.
>
> [PAUSE 10 SECONDS]
>
> Let every incoming breath bring life and energy, and every outgoing breath carry out the tension.
>
> [PAUSE 10 SECONDS]
>
> And let your heart beat slowly and evenly, slowly and evenly.
>
> [PAUSE 10 SECONDS]
>
> What words or pictures come to mind as you attend to your calm and even heartbeat? (Smith, 1989; p. 144)

Note, that as with Level I somatic focusing, unrestrictive instructions provide considerable leeway concerning the supportive words or pictures one selects. However, in a subtle and indirect way, Level II exercises are a bit more passive. Whereas most of the sensations targeted in Level I can be a byproduct of overt tensing or stretching (most people can actively generate an aftereffect of warmth and heaviness by squeezing or stretching muscles), for Level II this is less true. Few people can deliberately slow their heart, create sensations of warmth in the abdomen, or feel energy rising up the spine. Level II exercises also appear to require greater attentional focus. The target stimuli are subtle and internal, much more difficult to detect than sensations associated with the skin and musculature. One can also speculate that this level requires greater receptivity, given that the task of directing attention to one's heart, abdomen, or spinal cord, is the least familiar of all tasks we have considered to this point.

Thematic Imagery

Whereas somatic focusing is directed to physiological sensations, *thematic imagery* is entirely mental. One engages in a relatively unrestricted fantasy or daydream about a relaxing topic or theme, as illustrated below (Smith, 1989, p. 168):

> And now quietly ask yourself, "What scene or setting is most relaxing to me at the moment?"
> [PAUSE 10 SECONDS]
> You might want to picture a quiet beach, or a grassy plain, or a cool mountain top, or a peaceful pond.
> [PAUSE 10 SECONDS]
> Whatever scene or setting is most relaxing to you let it come to you in whatever way it wishes.
> [PAUSE 10 SECONDS]
> And now, quietly let your mind dwell on this scene for the next few seconds.
> [PAUSE 15 SECONDS]
> Let the scene become as vivid and real as possible.
> [PAUSE 10 SECONDS]
> How does it look?
> [PAUSE 10 SECONDS]
> Can you see the sky?
> [PAUSE]
> Can you feel the wind brushing against your skin?
> [PAUSE]
> Can you smell the gentle, cool air?
> [PAUSE]

Can you feel the warm sunlight or perhaps the cool night air?
[PAUSE]
Involve all your senses.

Somatic focusing and thematic imagery are both highly unrestrictive and passive approaches. However, it is difficult to make a case that imagery is any more or less focused, passive, or receptive than somatic focusing. It is true that some people have considerable difficulty visualizing, but then others find it quite easy. The justification for ranking thematic imagery after somatic focusing is in its capacity for supporting abstract and differentiated relaxation structures, as we shall see later in this chapter.

RESTRICTIVE MENTAL EXERCISES

Contemplation

Unlike somatic focusing and thematic imagery, restrictive approaches to relaxation define a highly limited attentional focus and permit few deviations. In addition to requiring considerable skill at focusing, they are highly passive. Virtually all attempts to actively direct or guide an exercise are considered to be diversions from the prime task of attending to the focal stimulus.

In the easiest restrictive approach, *contemplation*, one is given a target stimulus with the goal of generating associations. Employing a stance of "passive volition," one does not deliberately try to generate associations, although that is none the less the goal of the exercise. The objective is to passively obtain a richer and more complete appreciation of the focal stimulus. This is also the goal of Freud's free association and Gendlin's focusing exercises as well as advanced autogenic imagery in which one passively awaits "answers from the unconscious." In addition, a rich assortment of creativity exercises involve calmly and passively attending to an object of appreciation (a painting, piece of sculpture) or a question, and awaiting associations (Appendix A). Taken together, the term "contemplation" is a useful generic label for these exercises, although one must note that it is a word with quite different religious connotations for Hindus, Buddhists, and Christians.

Clearly, there is no limit to the possible objects of contemplation. In the following example, based on Gendlin's (1981) "focusing" exercise, one contemplates the meaning of relaxation itself (Smith, 1989, pp. 180–182):

In this exercise we are going to quietly attend to the experience of relaxation itself. . . .

[PAUSE]

Now ask yourself "What good thoughts and feelings are inside? What is the most relaxing feeling that comes to me right now?" Is it a body sensation? A state of mind? The feeling doesn't have to be anything big. It might be nothing more than a little feeling of calm or relief or a pleasant feeling in the body. There is nothing for you to figure out. Simply stay quiet and listen. Try not to hold on to any feeling or put it into words. Simply attend to any relaxing feeling that comes to you right now.

[PAUSE 5 SECONDS]

If no good or relaxing feeling comes to mind, you might want to think of a recent experience in which you felt good and were relaxed. Pick an experience that is fairly fresh to you, one that you can imagine clearly.

[PAUSE 10 SECONDS]

Imagine you are reexperiencing this pleasant and relaxing time.

[PAUSE]

What relaxing feeling comes to mind?

[PAUSE 20 SECONDS]

Now ask yourself, "What is the crux, the main thing about this good feeling?" And without trying to deliberately come up with an answer, simply relax and wait. See what words or pictures come from the good feeling.

[PAUSE 30 SECONDS]

Gently and easily direct your attention to the good, relaxing feeling. If it changes or moves, let it do that. Whatever the feeling does, follow and pay attention to it.

[PAUSE 10 SECONDS]

Note any words or pictures that might arise, and again and again gently return to attending to the good feeling.

[PAUSE 15 SECONDS]

Now what is fresh or new in what you feel? What is the crux, the main thing about your relaxed feeling?

[PAUSE 15 SECONDS]

How are the words or pictures changing? Let them change whatever way they want. There is nothing for you to do but attend to what is restful to you, and note the movement and evolution of your words or pictures—and return to the feeling.

[PAUSE 30 SECONDS]

From time to time quietly check your words or pictures.

[PAUSE 5 SECONDS]

Ask inside "Is that right? Do the words or pictures fit?" And without trying to figure anything out, simply and restfully wait and attend.

[PAUSE 15 SECONDS]

There is nothing for you to do except let the words or pictures change until they feel just right in capturing the gist of what is restful to you.

Note the differences between this exercise and imagery. In imagery, one is encouraged to attend and to dwell on a wide range of associations. Any related words or pictures that arise are legitimate focal stimuli. You may, while thinking about a peaceful forest, attend to the sky, the breeze, and then the smell of pines. However, in contemplation the attentional focus is much more restricted. The sky, tree, and pines, although desirable and enriching associations, must come and go. One dwells on no one association, but redirects attention, again and again, to the forest. Furthermore, during imagery you may take the role of director and actively modify your theme. The level of passivity required in contemplation does not permit such efforts.

Centered Focus Meditation

Popular forms of Western meditation, such as Benson's method and transcendental meditation, involve calmly restricting attention to a simple verbal stimulus such as a mantra, relaxing word, or count of breath (Appendix A). However, the range of useful meditative stimuli extends beyond such stimuli and include the flow of breath, rocking, or a simple visual image (Smith, 1986a). Taken together, such approaches can be generically termed *centered focus meditation.*

Centered focus meditation requires about the same level of focusing as contemplation. One begins by selecting a simple focal stimulus, calmly attending to it, and returning attention after every distraction. However, this form of meditation is more passive than contemplation. There is no indirect goal of evoking associations or acquiring a richer understanding of the meditation stimulus. All associations, indeed all expectations or attempts at "passive volition," represent unnecessary effort, distractions to be put aside. The simple passivity of centered focus meditation can be seen in the following example (Smith, 1989, pp. 193–194):

Now slowly let your mantra come to mind.

[PAUSE]

Let it come to you in whatever way it wishes.

[PAUSE]

Let it repeat, easily and effortlessly, like an echo, or clouds floating across the sky.

[PAUSE 5 SECONDS]

There is nothing for you to do but quietly attend to your mantra.

[PAUSE 15 SECONDS]

Every time your mind wanders or is distracted, that's OK. Gently and easily return to the mantra, again and again.

[PAUSE 10 SECONDS]

Let your mantra repeat effortlessly on its own for the next few minutes.

If this were a contemplation, the instructions might be "Calmly attend to your mantra. Let thoughts and images arise to give you a richer and more complete appreciation of your mantra. As each association emerges, gently put it aside, and await another. There is nothing you have to do but wait and appreciate the meanings your mantra has to offer." In centered focus meditation, even expectant waiting for illumination is too active. Put differently, if absolutely no associations emerge during meditation, fine. If no associations emerge during contemplation, then somehow the technique is not working.

Open Focus Meditation

Perhaps the most challenging form of meditation is variously called Zen *shikan-taza*, mindfulness, or *open focus meditation*. In these approaches, one quietly and calmly attends to, notes, and lets go of every stimulus that impinges upon awareness. One experiences every thought, feeling, or sensation without trying to figure it out, think about it, push it away, or do anything. One simply lets the stimulus come and go, and waits for the next one to come. Unlike contemplation, one does not nurture a sense of passive volition or expect that associations will be somehow meaningful. They may or may not. Unlike centered focus meditation, one does not even exert the minimal effort to choose or maintain attention on one stimulus. As can be seen in this example, one does not select a focal stimulus, but simply attends to all that spontaneously appear (Smith, 1989, pp. 195–196):

Now easily attend to every stimulus that comes to mind.

[PAUSE 5 SECONDS]

Every time you hear, think, or feel something, quietly acknowledge what you experience.

[PAUSE 5 SECONDS]

And let go of what you have noted, and return to attending to whatever stimulus drifts into consciousness.

[PAUSE 10 SECONDS]

There is nothing for you to do or figure out.

[PAUSE 10 SECONDS]

Quietly wait, like a still pond, for the next sound or thought. Note the ripple it makes in the stillness of your mind. Let the ripple settle, and quietly attend again.

[PAUSE 20 SECONDS]

There is nothing else for you to do but observe the flow of stimuli that, like clouds in the sky, or sounds in the night, come and go.

It is easy to confuse open focus meditation with thematic imagery fantasy or daydreaming. An important distinction between these approaches is that in imagery one attends to an experience that is more or less organized around a central theme, such as an outdoor scene. In addition, one makes some effort to involve all the senses. In open focus meditation, any attempt to select, organize, or elaborate one's experience would represent unnecessary and distracting effort. Indeed, it would be too active to even attempt to dwell on any one stimulus, no matter how enticing. In a sense, in open focus meditation, it is external stimuli that determine the course of meditation, not the meditator. For this reason, open focus meditation requires the greatest degree of receptivity. One must be willing, without exception, to tolerate and accept all stimuli that come to mind, no matter how unfamiliar, uncertain, or paradoxical.

ABSTRACTION/DIFFERENTIATION AND THE RELAXATION HIERARCHY

Our cognitive-behavioral model proposes that as one advances in relaxation, increasingly abstract and differentiated supportive structures are established. Restricted attitudes evolve into encompassing personal philosophies. Clearly, some approaches are more conducive to structure formation than others. If we examine the world's philosophical or religious literature, relatively little has been written on isometric squeeze or simple stretching exercises. In contrast, there is a vast literature on contemplation and meditation. A modest literature exists for breathing (pranayama traditions), somatic focusing (kundalini yoga), and imagery.

Is there something about simple squeezing that is not particularly conducive to lofty philosophical or religious thought? Why do virtually all world religious and many philosophical traditions have a central place for meditation? One reason may be that approaches to relaxation offer a varying range of useful symbols for expressing or representing abstract constructs. Exercises from isometric squeeze to somatic focusing incorporate prespecified physiological target stimuli, whether it be an act (squeezing, stretching, breathing), organ (muscle groups, heart), or sensation (warmth, heaviness). Such stimuli have somewhat restricted expressive value. For example, breathing exercises provide one symbol, the flow of air, which some traditions see as suggestive of life and energy (Iyengar, 1981). Somatic focusing provides a few additional symbols, somatic sensations, which some traditions view as chakras or "energy points" (Rama, Ballentine, & Ajaya, 1976). In contrast, imagery, contemplation, and meditation are not intrinsically linked with predefined target stimuli. Their foci can be selected to fit in with a philosophical or religious stance a rich variety of ways. One can attend to an image of the candle flame, the Virgin Mary, or the emptiness of space.

THE RELAXATION HIERARCHY AS AN IDEALIZED ABSTRACTION

We can see that there is perhaps a reason why relaxation systems around the world and throughout time have shown a remarkable consistency. The relaxation hierarchy identifies important differences among approaches in terms of focusing, passivity, receptivity, and abstraction/differentiation. Table 4.3 presents a composite ranking of our nine modalities of approaches on each of these dimensions.

However, our hierarchy is a highly idealized abstraction, a speculation suggested by, but not a necessary component of, the cognitive-behavioral model. Rarely in actual life are purified prototypical versions of exercises taught. Exercise blends are more typical. For example, attending to the word "one" while breathing out transforms a meditation to a combination meditation-breathing exercise, one difficult to rank. Holding a yoga stretch for a prolonged period of time introduces a

TABLE 4.3 Relaxation modalities ranked according to focusing, passivity, receptivity, and abstraction/differentiation

Approach	Focusing Rank	Passivity Rank	Receptivity Rank	Abstraction/ Differentiation Rank	Average rank
Isometric Squeeze Relaxation*	1	1	1	1	1.00
Yogaform Stretching	2	2	2 (?)	1	1.75
Breathing	3	3	3	1	2.50
Somatic Focusing I	3	4	3	1	2.75
Somatic Focusing II	4	5	4	1	3.50
Thematic Imagery	4	5	4 (?)	2	3.75
Contemplation	5	6	4	2	4.25
Centered Focus Meditation	5	7	4	2	4.50
Open Focus Meditation	5	8	5	2	5.00

*Note: Generic names are presented; rankings are based on purified prototypical instructions.

meditative component. Visualizing a peaceful breeze while breathing out blends imagery with breathing, and so on. Also, one can conceive of awkward or unusual versions of each approach that would appear misplaced in our hierarchy. Tensing and letting go of ocular muscles may require considerably more focusing than traditional isometric squeeze relaxation.

In addition, a variety of client factors may override the effects of an exercise's placement on the hierarchy. Belief in or prior experience with a technique, existing attitudes concerning relaxation, specific physical or emotional limitations, and environmental pressures can all contribute to preference for and responsivity to relaxation. Most important, one's current level of focusing, passivity, and receptivity may well determine which approaches are easy or difficult; a highly skilled individual may prefer meditation over isometric squeeze relaxation. Here it is important to note that attentional dimensions, such as focusing, appear to be independent from other aspects of personality and emotional functioning (Tellegen & Atkinson, 1974); a highly disturbed client may possess skills required for meditation whereas someone who is relatively integrated may be better suited for isometric squeeze relaxation.

Our relaxation hierarchy should be viewed as a conceptual tool, one that may reveal an implicit framework that has guided relaxation trainers for centuries. In practice, it is a provisional hypothesis that can guide our selection and evaluation of relaxation exercises. Most important, the hierarchy reminds us of important differences among approaches to relaxation. Different approaches may well work better for different people and treatment goals. If so, the popular strategy of teaching one or two techniques to all clients may not be sufficient.

THE UNIQUENESS OF RELAXATION PROCEDURES

We have seen that relaxation procedures differ in terms of the skills and structures required and evoked. In addition, exercises may differ considerably on any of the numerous subordinate convergent and divergent processes that contribute to the relaxation cycle (habituation, oxygenation of the blood, somatic relaxation sensations, etc.). Taken together, skills, structures, and subordinate processes combine to give each approach to relaxation a unique identity or "personality." The novice relaxer may be unable to differentiate the effects of isometric squeeze relaxation, breathing, or meditation, just as the novice cook may be unable to differentiate the subtleties of different cuisines. However, an experienced relaxer, like a seasoned cook, can appreciate and articulate subtle nuances among approaches. Isometric squeeze relaxation may be experienced as "soothing, warm, tingling, mellow," breathing exercises, "invigorating, light, refreshing," meditation, "centered, focused, clear," and so on. Relaxation, like art, music, or literature, offers a rainbow of riches to those who become masters of their craft.

CHAPTER 5

The Instruction of
Cognitive-Behavioral Relaxation

Relaxation training must do more than reduce arousal. We have seen that additional cognitive-behavioral goals include the development of focusing, passivity, and receptivity as well as beliefs, values, and commitments conducive to relaxation. In terms of our model, the relaxation instructor should attempt to facilitate relaxation skill mastery and cognitive restructuring cycles.

THE DEVELOPMENT OF SKILLS AND STRUCTURES

Skill Shaping

Traditional approaches to relaxation often impose a single technique on all clients. Whether it be progressive relaxation or meditation, the client is told to practice regularly if results are desired. If a technique is boring or ineffective, a therapist may fine-tune specific exercises or recommend continued practice. I propose that it may be more useful to start with exercises matched to a client's level of skill and proceed in easily managed steps.

The relaxation hierarchy, although an idealized abstraction, suggests a variety of skill-shaping strategies. Approaches appearing low on the hierarchy, such as isometric squeeze relaxation and yoga stretching, may require less skill than meditation and contemplation. If so, and when teaching several exercises, it would make sense to begin with easier exercises and progress to those that are more difficult. This, as we have seen, is the strategy of virtually every relaxation system that incorporates combinations of exercises. Furthermore, clients having difficulty with high ranked approaches might be advised to attempt approaches lower on the hierarchy.

Shaping can be introduced into a single relaxation sequence. For example, if a decision has been made to proceed with a relatively difficult approach, one could begin with "warm-up" exercises selected from lower on the hierarchy. Such exercises may serve to enhance focusing, passivity, and receptivity so that relaxation might proceed with less difficulty. Similarly, if a client desires to include a variety of exercises in one session (yoga, imagery, and meditation, e.g.), it would make sense to present them in the order suggested by our idealized hierarchy (or in the order of ease and familiarity to the client).

Articulation

As we have noted, articulation involves identifying and finding labels (words or images) for a relaxation experience. At the simplest level this involves noting sources of tension that may be present ("Attend to the tightness in your shoulders."). Once articulated, a client can work to let go of tension. In addition, a client can be assisted in articulating experiences associated with relaxation. Most often these include somatic sensations ("I feel warm and heavy.") and manifestations of focusing, passivity, and receptivity ("I feel centered, free, open."). It should be noted that a rich array of somatic and skill-related relaxation experiences are possible (see Table 3.4). Once articulated, tension can be differentiated from relaxation (as in progressive relaxation) and deeper levels of relaxation from each other.

Articulation is a symbol-making process that can be enhanced in a variety of ways. Checklists (Tables 3.3 and 3.4) describing relaxation states can be presented before or after a relaxation session. Guiding instructor "patter" that accompanies an exercise can incorporate relaxation words. Clients can be asked to identify and describe everyday relaxation experiences that resemble those that appear in the practice session. Even Gendlin's (1981) "focusing" exercise, an association technique for uncovering the "felt meanings" of a problem, can be used to explore the experience of relaxation (Smith, 1989).

Relaxation Appraisals and Cognitive Restructuring

Cognitive-behavioral relaxation training emphasizes the acquisition of beliefs, values, and commitments supportive of relaxation. This can occur at many levels. First, clinicians often inadvertently contribute to

an aversive form of cognitive restructuring. For example, a desensitization regimen that matches an incompletely mastered relaxation exercise with an aversive stimulus risks introducing aversive appraisals to
relaxation. Clinicians who encourage regular exercise practice exclusively through exhortations and lectures also risk evoking frustration
and negative relaxation appraisals.

Finally, inappropriate instructions can also contribute to negative
appraisals of relaxation. A clinician whose instructions suggest "Let
your muscles *completely* relax, enjoy the pleasant sensations of *complete* relaxation" risks worrying clients about a level of relaxation few
will be able to achieve. A preferable instruction is not only realistic, but
describes what happens in relaxation. One might say "Let your muscles
begin to relax, enjoy the pleasant sensations as relaxation *begins to* take
place." The process of relaxation is such that it takes time to release
tension. In summary, cognitive restructuring begins by avoiding procedural mistakes that can lead to aversive treatment appraisals.

More formally, cognitive restructuring can be introduced as a component of relaxation training. A client must not only find proper symbols
(words or pictures) for relaxation experiences, but decide if these
experiences can be supported by his or her beliefs, values, and commitments. In most general terms, this involves asking three basic questions:

1. Belief Questions: Are my relaxation experiences real and not an
artifact of a dream or drug-induced state? Are they of potentially lasting
impact, and under my control? What do they mean in the context of my
global beliefs concerning the course of relaxation? What beliefs concerning interpersonal relationships, work, leisure, as well as the ultimate nature of myself and the universe interfere with or support
relaxation?
2. Value Questions: Are my relaxation experiences worth anything? Are
they good for me? Are they just signs of idleness, laziness, and needless
self-indulgence? What are the most important goals and ideals in my life
and how do they support or interfere with relaxation?
3. Commitment Questions: What am I willing to give up, i.e., time,
convenience, and comfort, in order to practice? Am I willing to practice
regularly? Am I willing to examine basic beliefs and actions that may not
be consistent with relaxation? Have I committed myself to activities
outside of relaxation that may support or interfere with relaxation?

Lets take a look at how these questions might be answered by a
beginning, intermediate, and advanced relaxer. For a beginning relaxer,
answers might include:

It used to be I couldn't tell when I was tense. Now I know what muscle tension feels like, and how it's different from muscle relaxation. I feel "comfortable" and "soothed" when relaxing, just like after a massage. I believe that when I feel comfortable and soothed, it is because I have evoked a "relaxation response" that is the mirror image of the stress "flight-or-fight response." I also believe that I have the power to extend these feelings into everyday life. I value these feelings; they are important to my health. And I am willing to give up 30 minutes every day to practice relaxation.

An intermediate relaxer might have a slightly different set of answers:

When relaxing, I escape into a private fantasy world, a special image of a pond I call my "escape place." Sometimes I get distracted by a pleasant daydream about my new car, or simply by pleasurable physical sensations. I now recognize these as distractions, not the same as my special escape place, and return to my image. In addition, I believe that answers to private problems and concerns can come to me in such a place. These answers are not just daydreams, but creative options. I value and treasure my escape place, just as I treasure my own hometown. Not only am I willing to practice daily, but I feel it is important to act on, or at least take seriously, answers that come to me in my escape place.

An advanced relaxer may have quite different answers:

I relax by attending to my meditative stimulus, a simple prayer I learned when I was a child. When doing this, my mind feels "centered" and "at one." These feelings are not the same as fantasy or daydreaming; in fact, when I lapse into fantasy, I recognize that I am no longer meditating and return to my simple prayer. I believe my meditation can teach me profound lessons about the meaning of life; I value and trust my meditation, much as I would trust a dear friend. And I make every attempt to live my life according to insights I have learned from meditation. I take care of my body through proper diet and exercise. I share my love with others. Most important, I live one day at a time.

It is important to realize that each individual at each level of relaxation has his or her own questions and answers. They can be as simple as deciding to practice regularly, or once a week. They can be as profound as communing with God, or encountering the vast emptiness of being.

Whatever the level of training, the extent to which a relaxation instructor can clarify and facilitate such questioning can do much to enhance growth in relaxation. A rich array of cognitive-behavioral tools are available, including brainstorming, listing priorities, "empty chair" dialogues, daily diaries, testing out acceptable commitments with homework assignments, direct challenging of beliefs, covertly rehearsing rational and adaptive self-statements, and the like (Ellis & Grieger, 1977; Meichenbaum, 1977; Mullen, 1986).

Once identified, affirmations of relaxation beliefs, values, and commitments can be woven into a relaxation sequence.

DEEPENING STRATEGIES

Deepening Phrases

One powerful adjunct to relaxation is to incorporate strategies designed to enhance the deepening of relaxation. This can be achieved by incorporating in instructions phrases suggesting enhancement of relaxation skills or somatic sensations that may already have been articulated. Note that here the suggestions do not simply restate experiences, but suggest a change in the direction of increased relaxation ("You are becoming more focused." rather than "Let yourself feel how focused you are."). Some examples might include:

> Let yourself feel warmer and heavier. *(somatic sensation)*
>
> Let tingling sensations begin to flow over your body. *(somatic sensation)*
>
> You are becoming more centered. *(focusing)*
>
> Your mind is more attentive. *(focusing)*
>
> Practice with increasing ease and effortlessness. *(passivity)*
>
> Let yourself experience more and more deeply a state of "letting be." *(passivity)*
>
> You feel increasingly open to possibilities. *(receptivity)*
>
> You can trust more and more the hidden processes of relaxation. *(receptivity)*

A skilled relaxation trainer can enhance relaxation by suggesting experiences that start with and go slightly beyond what the client is experiencing. For example, at the end of a brief relaxation demonstration, a client may report that the trainer's voice seemed to "move a few feet away and become slightly quieter." If a full relaxation session were to follow this demonstration, the trainer might build on this experience by suggesting "as you sink deeper and deeper into relaxation, my voice moves further into the distance, so far that it can barely be heard." A trainer might note somatic changes often indicative of relaxation processes (drooping eyelids, slower breathing, slightly open jaws) and weave these into deepening suggestions ("As you become relaxed your eyelids become heavy, so heavy you can barely keep them open" . . . "As you settle into relaxation, your breathing begins to slow, it becomes very even and regular" . . . "As you let go of tension your jaws begin to loosen and relax"). In these examples somatic suggestions not only reflect physiological changes that may be occurring, but point to future related changes that may occur as relaxation progresses.

On the structural level, relaxation can be deepened by including affirmations that relaxation beliefs, values, and commitments will be experienced more deeply ("It's OK to put aside past and future concerns and attend to the task at hand." . . . "Let yourself become more open to the powers within."). A somewhat more complex strategy involves weaving in components of beliefs, values, and commitments to reflect increasing levels of abstraction and differentiation. To elaborate, a cognitive structure can be viewed as itself having a structure, a hierarchical *configuration* of associated beliefs, values, and commitments. Components or derivatives of a structure can be introduced throughout an exercise, starting with those that are restricted and concrete, and ending with those that are most encompassing, as illustrated below:

> Tense and let go of each muscle group. Let go of the tension you have created.
>
> There is no need for you effortfully strive to be relaxed.
>
> Simply let relaxation happen as you let go of tension.
>
> Live in the present moment. Let go of your concerns over that which cannot be changed.

In this example "Let go of your concerns over that which cannot be changed" is an abstract structure. "Let relaxation happen" and "Tense and let go of each muscle group" are progressively concrete manifestations of this structure.

Deepening Imagery

A different deepening strategy is to introduce imagery that changes in a direction of increased focus, passivity, and receptivity. Note how the following imagery is initially complex and active, and then becomes more focused, passive, and receptive:

You are on a quiet beach. As you sit up and look around, you notice the blue water and sky. The sun is directly overhead, its warm rays dissolving tension in your body. You can feel a breeze and hear the soothing waves splash against the shore. As you become more relaxed, you recline on the beach. Your attention narrows to the sky above, and the peaceful clouds floating by. There is nothing you have to think about or do. Simply attend to the clouds and nothing else. All sorts of thoughts and images may come to mind, and that's OK. Simply let them come and go, and return your attention to the graceful clouds.

Deepening Transitions

If more than one general exercise approach is selected, deepening transitions can be introduced between each approach. Such transitions reinforce the appraisal that the sequence is not an arbitrary assortment of exercises, but a progression moving into deeper and deeper levels of relaxation. Thus, if a trainee has selected both isometric squeeze and yogaform stretching exercises, the transition between both approaches might read:

We have now completed one approach to relaxation. We will now move on to another set of exercises many find even more deeply satisfying. As we try these exercises, let yourself become more and more fully relaxed.

Deepening Metaphors

The skilled use of metaphor can enhance relaxation processes. Metaphors can symbolize both concrete exercise procedures and abstract cognitive structures. A swaying tree can signify a yoga stretch or the philosophical affirmation, "Flow with the here and now." Crashing ocean waves can signify the exhalation of breath, or a commitment, "Let go of that which cannot be changed." Such metaphors are in a sense more abstract than exercises, and more concrete than cognitive structures. Since they exist at an intermediate level of abstraction, they can be used to foster transitions from concrete conceptualizations of relaxation to more encompassing cognitive structures. This is illustrated in the highly truncated sequence below.

Stretch and unstretch your arms . . .

Stretch and unstretch your legs . . .

With each stretch you are like a tree swaying in the wind . . .

Stretch, unstretch, and sway in the wind . . .

A tree sways in the wind, firmly rooted in the earth, yet flowing with the moment.

Remember how you, firmly supported by the ground of life, can flow with the moment.

Relaxation Countdown

One way to enhance relaxation is to introduce a relaxation countdown. One starts with any number, usually 5 or 10, and slowly counts back to 0. Each count is associated with deeper levels of relaxation. To do a countdown, first explain the procedure, as illustrated here:

I will begin to count backwards from 5 to 0.

With each count, let yourself become more and more relaxed.

Then start counting. Between each number introduce a few relaxing phrases. Such a countdown can be introduced in isometric squeeze relaxation, breathing, and imagery. For example, an isometric squeeze relaxation countdown would begin at the onset of each "let go" cycle:

Tense up.

And let go.

We begin with 5.

Attend to the sensations of relaxation.

4

Let the tension slowly begin to flow out of

your muscles.

3

Notice the difference between tension and relaxation.

2

Let your muscles become more and more fully relaxed.

1

Let go of any feelings of tension you may feel.

And 0.

Countdowns can be woven into virtually any approach to relaxation. For example, in stretching and breathing sequences, they can be incorporated with unstretching and exhalation. Imagery provides the richest opportunity for countdown relaxation. Here the actual content of an image can change to symbolize increased focusing, passivity, and receptivity with each count. This is illustrated by the following image of floating into the clouds:

> You are resting on earth and become so relaxed that you begin to float.
>
> 5
>
> As you let go of your tensions, you become lighter and lighter.
>
> 4
>
> Your mind centers on the peaceful sensations of floating and relaxation.
>
> 3
>
> You float higher and higher. The houses and trees below become smaller and smaller. Your everyday pressures and concerns seem so distant.
>
> 2
>
> As you approach the peaceful soft clouds, your mind feels more and more free, more open to the possibilities of relaxation.
>
> 1
>
> You float into the clouds, completely without effort or concern. You settle into a deep and comfortable state of relaxation.
>
> And 0.

ANTICIPATION OF SETBACK

In relaxation training, a legion of setbacks are possible: attention wanders; expected relaxation effects do not occur; unexpected experiences are encountered; one forgets to practice; maladaptive thoughts interfere with relaxation; coping failures in everyday life increase tension; relaxation beliefs, values, and commitments are forgotten, and so on. Early in training, a client can be taught to expect such setbacks and develop appropriate appraisals (for example, "Distractions are normal, and can indicate that relaxation is uncovering hidden stresses;" "Relaxation is like any other skill, it takes time to work;" "Sometimes deeper levels of relaxation can create unexpected feelings and sensations").

In addition, one can plan ahead coping strategies for dealing with setback (Meichenbaum, 1977, 1985). Once procedure, *cycle-enhancing imagery* (Smith, 1986a) anticipates potential setbacks by: (a) implicitly acknowledging that relaxation involves a cyclical process with divergent and convergent phases, and (b) affirming the redeployment of focusing, passivity, and receptivity. Examples include:

> Whenever you notice you are thinking about something unrelated to relaxation, picture yourself letting go of this thought as if it were a butterfly you are holding and releasing.
>
> Give each distracting thought to your relaxation as if you were giving it a gift.
>
> Say to yourself, "What an interesting distraction. OK, back to my relaxation."
>
> Say to the distraction "thank you" and return to your exercise.
>
> Imagine dropping each distraction into a deep space as though you were dropping pebbles into a pond.
>
> Let distracting thoughts and pictures stay in your mind if they want. But they stay in the background while you return to your exercise.
>
> Imagine each distraction to be a form of stress release that enables you to relax better.

REINFORCEMENT OF RELAXATION

In teaching and presenting relaxation, it is important to introduce a few words of encouragement and support and highlight pleasurable experiences as well as a client's strengths and capacities. At one level, such reinforcements can reward and strengthen such relaxation behavior as regular practice, the consistent deployment of relaxation skills, and affirmations of relaxation structures. In addition, they can contribute to convergent restructuring, that is, the development of new structures supportive of positive experiences associated with lowered arousal and increased deployment of focusing, passivity, and receptivity.

Relaxation reinforcements can be presented as direct statements ("Very good.") or as phrases combined with other instructions ("It is good to let go of the cares of the day.") Some reinforcing phrases include (for a lexicon of potentially reinforcing words, see Table 3.4):

> There is no need to push yourself, you are doing fine.
>
> Move at a pace that feels comfortable to you.
>
> Notice the pleasant feelings you have created.
>
> It's OK to let yourself sink deeper into relaxation.
>
> Every minute you let go and attend to relaxation, you are doing well.
>
> It feels good to let tension go.

It is important not to introduce reinforcements for thoughts and behaviors that may not be present. For example, the reinforcement, "It is good that you are completely relaxed." may actually create needless worry and tension if one is not in fact completely relaxed. It is better to reinforce relaxation attempts ("It is good to begin to put aside the cares of the day.") as well as the general direction (and not end point) of relaxation ("It is good to become more focused.").

Reinforcement should be withheld from thoughts and behaviors not conducive to relaxation. For example, it's OK to experience distraction during a session. However, pursing distractions for any length of time serves to reinforce the initial decision to pursue. Also, by reacting to distraction with a considerable degree of disturbance and upset, one appraises the distraction as major and important. It is better to treat distractions as passing and insignificant.

GENERALIZATION STRATEGIES

Once mastered, a relaxation technique can be incorporated into a variety of therapeutic regimens designed to foster generalization of relaxation to life at large. For example, in traditional desensitization, a client relaxes while being exposed to a hierarchy of anxiety-arousing stimuli (Wolpe, 1958). Through reciprocal inhibition each stimulus eventually ceases to evoke anxiety, and relaxation generalizes. When cognitive-behavioral relaxation is used with desensitization, structure affirmations can be introduced into a relaxation sequence that serve the dual purpose of supporting relaxation as well as effective and realistic coping. For example, a client undergoing treatment for test anxiety might practice relaxation while imagining a test-taking situation. The relaxation sequence might include the following phrase: "As you breathe out, let go of tension. Put your past and future concerns aside. Attend the present moment." This statement not only affirms a relaxation-supporting structure, but is consistent with self-statements directed towards coping with a test ("There is no need to worry about the past or future while taking this test. Simply attend to one question at a time").

In addition, generalization can be fostered through special exercises directed towards identifying manifestations of focusing, passivity, and receptivity in everyday activities. Clients can be encouraged through targeted homework exercises to note when at work they were "most focused" or successful at "putting unnecessary worry or distracting tasks aside." In addition, homework assignments can specify certain tasks to be completed "in the spirit of focusing, passivity, and receptivity." For example, a housewife who gardens might be encouraged to set aside one hour a day to simply tend to the garden and nothing else. The effect of these supplementary exercises can be to reinforce the concepts of focusing, passivity, and receptivity, highlight their potential manifestation in everyday life, and set the stage for generalization of relaxation beyond the practice session.

Generalization can be further enhanced by abbreviating relaxation exercises so they can be practiced in a variety of settings. One traditional way of doing this is through "cue-controlled relaxation." Here, a relaxation cue word, such as "calm," is systematically matched with a relaxation exercise so that eventually the word is sufficient to evoke relaxation. In a cognitive-behavioral version of this approach, *conceptual cue words* additionally summarize a client's appraisal of relaxation. For example, if a client thinks of isometric squeeze relaxation as "a way of letting go of the burdens of unnecessary muscle tension," the phrase "let go" would be an appropriate conceptual cue. A religiously inclined client who appraises meditative relaxation as "a way of putting aside my narrow, selfish worries and following the broader word of God" might use the cue "God's will be done." Unlike traditional cue words, conceptual cue words derive their effect both through association with relaxation and their appraised meaning.

The *conceptual mini-relaxation* is an extended version of conceptual cue-controlled relaxation. Here, highlights most representative or symbolic of an exercise sequence are incorporated into a brief exercise. For example, an entire exercise sequence might consist of: (a) a series of deep breathing and stretching exercises followed by (b) five minutes of tensing up while inhaling and letting go while exhaling and ending with (c) five minutes of escape imagery focusing on the theme "floating in the clouds." The key elements of this sequence can be summarized and symbolized by the following mini-relaxation: "Tense up and breathe in . . . and let go of tension while exhaling, visualizing your tension floating away into the clouds."

SETTING UP A RELAXATION PROGRAM

Cognitive-behavioral principles can be incorporated in any relaxation program, ranging from progressive relaxation and autogenic training to imagery and meditation (see Appendices B and C for suggestions). However, it is perhaps better not to view cognitive-behavioral relaxation training as a system to replace others, but as a global way of conceptualizing all of relaxation. It is in this spirit that we consider in the following chapter some general principles for effective relaxation training.

CHAPTER 6

Coherence and Integrity: The Science and Art of Relaxation

COHERENCE

The relaxation strategies we have just considered are designed to contribute to the external objectives of skill and structure development. A different type of objective, one rarely considered in relaxation texts, is the overall internal coherence of an exercise sequence. Let us define *procedural coherence* as the degree of interrelatedness among specific exercise components and *conceptual coherence* as the interrelatedness of associations or meanings ascribed to these components. For example, consider the following two sequences:

Sequence 1
Squeeze and let go of your shoulders (isometric squeeze relaxation).

Attend to the sensations of letting go.

Take a deep breath and exhale.

Slowly stretch your arms over your head (yoga stretch).

Now, squeeze and let go of your hands (isometric squeeze relaxation).

Sequence 2
Take a deep breath.

Now squeeze your shoulders, and as you let go, easily exhale.

Lets try a more gentle version of this exercise with the hands.

> Take a deep breath and make a tight fist.
>
> Then, let go as you slowly exhale.
>
> Now for an exercise that is even more gentle.
>
> Slowly inhale as you stretch your arms over your head, and exhale as you return your arms to your sides.

The first exercise lacked procedural coherence. The four exercise elements (shoulder squeeze, deep breathing, arm stretch, hand squeeze) are a more or less random sequence of calisthenics. The second sequence shows greater internal structure. Exercises flow from active to relatively passive. The breathing exercise is logically integrated into each component. The two squeezing exercises (shoulder and hand) are presented side by side.

Now let's examine two more sequences, the first lacking conceptual coherence:

> Imagine you are a leaf, calmly floating on the surface of a still pond.
>
> Let your mind dwell on this peaceful mental image.
>
> Now, tightly squeeze your arms, bending them at the elbow, and *let go.*
>
> Attend to the sensations of letting go.
>
> You sink deeper into relaxation.
>
> Let yourself breathe fully and deeply, and attend to the rush of air, flowing like a firm, gentle breeze, carrying out your tensions.

This sequence could become rather frightening if one examines the meanings and associations that might be triggered by each element. We begin with perfectly fine mental image, a leaf floating on a calm pond. However, the subsequent vigorous isometric squeeze exercise is inconsistent with the degree of calm that might be established by the image. Even worse, squeezing and letting go could transform the delicate floating image into a wet disaster (one can easily picture the poor leaf desperately thrashing and sinking). The associations of the next component, "sink deeper," are hardly pleasant thoughts for a floating, or sinking, leaf. The element, "Breathe fully and deeply . . . like a firm gentle breeze," not only makes no sense if one has sunk into the pond, but is even inconsistent if one has survived the associations of the isometric squeeze relaxation exercise and is still floating on the pond's "calm surface." This sequence is clearly a disaster of incongruent images and potential associations. Now examine a sequence that is more successful, one also incorporating aquatic imagery, isometric squeeze relaxation, and breathing.

Imagine you are a leaf on a tree overlooking a small pond.

Squeeze your arm and hand muscles.

As you let go, imagine, you are letting go of the tree.

You touch and float on the pond's surface.

A slight breeze stirs the surface of the water.

As you gently and peacefully rock, your breath quietly flows with the rhythm of your movement.

Gently in, gently out, with each breath your tensions flow and rock away.

Note how the explicit images are congruous with each exercise component (squeezing and letting go, a leaf falling from a tree; floating in the breeze and on the surface of a pond, slowly breathing in and out). Note how each image flows logically from the next (actively falling, passively floating) and how this progression is paralleled by physical exercise elements (active squeeze, passive breathing).

Coherence serves a number of functions. Sequences are more likely to be remembered, since they form larger conceptual "chunks." More important, a coherent sequence has built in a sophisticated series of discriminative stimuli, linked to relaxation in general and to each step relaxation takes. Such stimuli, established either through pairing (as in cue-controlled relaxation), or because of their conceptual and formal link to subsequent relaxation, not only serve to unify a relaxation sequence but provide a variety of cues that can signal or evoke relaxation outside of the practice session.

A number of specific strategies can be used to enhance coherence.

Procedural Integration

If a trainee's relaxation sequence includes more than one general approach (e.g., yoga stretching, breathing, and imagery), elements of one approach can be integrated into others. For example, breathing exercises can be separately featured in a relaxation sequence or woven into isometric squeeze relaxation and yoga stretching:

Take a deep breath as you tighten up the muscles.

Hold the muscles tighter and tighter.

And as you let go, gently exhale.

Now, slowly, smoothly, and gently stretch.

Stretch farther and farther.

Gently take in a deep breath as you stretch completely.

And very slowly, smoothly, and gently release the stretch, while easily exhaling.

Similarly, if a client demonstrates proficiency at imagery, specific images symbolizing focusing, passivity, and receptivity can be integrated into other approaches, such as isometric squeeze relaxation, yoga stretching, and breathing:

As you let go of your tension, imagine a tight ball of string slowly unwinding. Bit by bit each string relaxes as you let go of tension more and more completely. Gently and easily the entire wad becomes more and more loose.

As you stretch, imagine you are a tree. Your arms are the branches gracefully bending in the wind. With every breeze, you bend, and release your tensions.

You are by the seashore. As each wave approaches the shore you take a deep breath. As the wave splashes against the shore, you gently exhale and release your tensions.

Framing Elements

An element that appears at the onset of a sequence can be repeated at the end. The end version may be modified to reflect increased focus, passivity, and receptivity. For example, a set of exercises might begin with the image of a unsettled pond, its wind-blown surface symbolizing distraction and unnecessary effortful striving. An appropriate ending could be a still, quiet pond. Similarly, one might begin and end a sequence with a deep breathing exercise. The initial exercise might be performed with some vigor and effort whereas the final version would be conducted with greater calm.

Metaphor

We have noted earlier how the use of metaphors can foster the abstraction/differentiation process. In addition, metaphors can interrelate and summarize procedural and conceptual components of an exercise and provide subtle transitions between exercises. For example, initially a yoga sequence might be described as similar to a tree bending in a wind. Later on, actual stretching instructions might be replaced with a summarizing metaphor; the relaxer stretches to the instructions "You are a tree bending in a wind . . . bending slowly, smoothly, and gently." Eventually, the same metaphor can serve as a cue for a mental imagery sequence, "Imagine in your mind a tree bending . . ." When metaphor is woven into an exercise sequence, it can serve not only as a unifying and transitional device, but as a recurring cue or reminder that the exercise sequence is becoming increasingly cognitive and passive.

INTEGRITY

The *integrity* of an exercise sequence is the extent to which component elements contribute to an overall, unifying idea. A unifying idea consists of a rationale, goal, affirmation, metaphor, or story that defines an exercise. It can be in the client's own words, or embodied in a passage from a song, poem, prayer, or piece of literature the client has found to be particularly peaceful. Whatever its form the unifying idea is what a sequence is all about, its justification.

Often, a unifying idea is little more than the rationale provided by the relaxation trainer. For example, a practitioner of progressive relaxation (Bernstein & Borkovec, 1973) would probably think of each exercise enhancing ability to discriminate and let go of tension. A practitioner of Benson's "breathing-one" meditation might view the technique as a device for triggering the relaxation response.

A relaxation goal can be simply the pragmatic reason for practicing relaxation, for example: "stress release," "combating insomnia," "waking up refreshed for the day," "preparing for work," or even "prayer" or "communing with nature." A goal can also be artistic expression. Here, constructing or practicing an exercise becomes a special and somewhat unusual art form, one with the dual goals of creating a thing of beauty and evoking relaxation. Put differently, techniques of relaxation become an expressive medium, analogous to the words of a poet, the paints of an artist, or the dance steps of a choreographer.

Unifying ideas can be affirmations of specific relaxation structures, for example, "Live in the present moment," "God's will be done," "Let go of that which cannot be changed," or "Trust the powers within you."

They can be symbolic representations or metaphors of what relaxation means to the client. The theme of a *peaceful woods* might symbolize many aspects of a relaxation sequence. For example, a gentle breeze might symbolize breathing exercises; trees slowly bowing in the wind, stretching exercises; the sun warming the leaves, somatic "warmth and heaviness"; and the silence of approaching evening, a meditative focus of attention. Note how these images are not only peaceful in their own right, but suggestive of specific relaxation exercises. To take an example presented later in this book, the theme of *waves crashing on the shore* can symbolize a variety of exercises. The energy that builds and releases with each crashing wave can suggest the tension-release cycle of isometric squeeze relaxation (or inhalation and exhalation of deep breathing). The dissolving of each wave into the sand can be linked with somatic focusing suggestions of "heaviness, tingling, and dissolving tension." And the quiet wind that flows across the water before the next wave can suggest focused breathing.

A unifying idea can be something of a very simple story or changing metaphor, providing all elements are linked to relaxation exercises, change in a direction of increased relaxation, and end in deeper relaxation. For example, the theme of waves crashing on the shore just mentioned is a bit of a story—a wave builds up, crashes, dissolves into the sand, and a quiet wind blows. A relaxation story must also be very simple, for example, lighting a fireplace and reclining on a sofa, slowly floating on a ship out to sea, or walking deeper into a quiet forest.

Whatever its form, a unifying idea can contribute considerably to the structure and meaning of a relaxation sequence and link relaxation to a client's beliefs, values, and commitments. It provides a criterion for selecting, ordering, elaborating, and refining exercises as well as for introducing coherence. As such, a unifying idea contributes to the integrity of a relaxation sequence. To see how this can occur, examine the following sequence lacking integrity:

[ISOMETRIC SQUEEZE RELAXATION]

Make a fist with your right hand.

Let your muscles become tight and hard.

Notice the sensations of tension.

And *let go.*

Let the tension flow.

Notice the sensations of relaxation you have created.

Let your fingers and hands become soft and warm, soft and heavy.

[REPEAT FOR MAJOR MUSCLE GROUPS]

[BREATHING]

Now, attend to your breathing.

Let each breath become slow, smooth, and full.

Become more calm and centered.

Let each outgoing breath begin to dissolve the tensions of the day.

And let the stream of breath gently flow.
[CONTINUE BREATHING EXERCISE FOR 5 MINUTES]
[IMAGERY]

Gently let yourself continue breathing in whatever way feels comfortable and easy.

You are in a quiet cabin by the lake.

A burning candle reveals a soft and comfortable chair.

The walls are a rich, warm wood.

In front of the candle is a large window and beyond the flame's gentle reflection in the glass you can see shadows of trees bending easily in the wind.

The sun is beginning to set and the world grows more still.

Let yourself become immersed in this setting with all your senses.

What relaxing sounds do you hear?

The outside breeze?

A distant bird?

The quiet flicker of the candle flame?

What relaxing scents can you smell?

The wood of the cabin?

Apple cider cooking on the stove?

The soothing pine scent released by the burning candle?

Quietly attend to this relaxing place with all your senses.
[PAUSE 5 MINUTES]

[MEDITATION]

Easily let go of what you are attending to.

Gently focus on your breathing.

With every outgoing breath, count "one."

This is your meditation for the next five minutes.
[PAUSE 5 MINUTES]

Compare this sequence with a parallel one possessing greater integrity:

[ISOMETRIC SQUEEZE RELAXATION]
Picture tension as a hard ball of candle wax.

Frozen within are the cares and hassles of the day.

Now, take a deep breath make a fist with your right hand.

Let your muscles become as tight as hard wax.

Notice the sensations of tension.

And *let go* and exhale.

Imagine the candle is lit.

Let the tension flow as the wax by the flame begins to melt.

Notice the sensations of relaxation you have created.

Let your fingers and hands become soft and warm, soft and heavy

As the wax begins to flow and release its tensions.

[REPEAT FOR MAJOR MUSCLE GROUPS]

[BREATHING]

Let each breath become slow, smooth, and full.

As you become more calm and centered, imagine the delicate dance of the candle flame.

Let each outgoing breath begin to dissolve the tensions of the day

And let the stream of breath gently flow past the candle flame

Barely enough to make it flicker.

[CONTINUE BREATHING EXERCISE FOR 5 MINUTES]

[IMAGERY]

Gently let yourself continue breathing in whatever way feels comfortable and easy.

You are able to let the cares of the day become more and more distant.

Direct your attention to the glowing candle.

And the peaceful setting its flickering light reveals.

You are in a quiet cabin by the lake.

The candle reveals a soft and comfortable chair.

The walls are a rich, warm wood.

In front of the candle is a large window and beyond the flame's gentle reflection in the glass you can see shadows of trees bending easily in the wind.

The sun is beginning to set and the world grows more still.

Let yourself become immersed in this setting with all your senses.

What relaxing sounds do you hear?

The outside breeze?

A distant bird?

The quiet flicker of the candle flame?

What relaxing scents can you smell?

The wood of the cabin?

Apple cider cooking on the stove?

The soothing pine scent released by the burning candle?

Quietly attend to this relaxing place with all your senses.

[PAUSE 5 MINUTES]

[MEDITATION]

Easily let go of what you are attending to.

Evening has come.

Let your breath become so still that it can barely be noticed.

Your cares and concerns seem so small and distant in the immense peace that blankets the world.

You can rest secure that the flame of life continues on its own.

It's OK to let yourself settle into a deep inner clam.

Become more and more focused on the delicate candle flame.

The air is still and the flame burns calmly and silently.

Gently attend to the flame.

Whenever your mind wanders, that's OK.

Gently return to the silent flame.

This is your meditation for the next five minutes.

[PAUSE 5 MINUTES]

Note that both exercise sequences contain the same components: isometric squeeze, breathing, imagery, and centered focus meditation. Both could be performed in the same length of time (about 30 minutes). However, the second sequence has considerable integrity (as well as coherence). Each component is tied to the unifying idea of a candle. The metaphors of melting wax and the burning flame first symbolize concrete exercise components (isometric squeeze relaxation, breathing), and then reflect a more encompassing relaxation structure ("Your cares and concerns seem so small and distant in the immense peace that blankets the world. You can rest secure that the flame of life continues on its own."). Procedural components and imagery content become progressively more focused and passive, enhanced by deepening suggestions ("calm, centered . . . cares of the day become more and more distant . . . still . . . become immersed . . . become more and more focused"). Breathing is not only woven into every segment as a unifying element, but itself becomes more focused and passive. Finally, the sequence is framed by the image of a candle, first the unlit wax, and then the flame.

THE ART AND SCIENCE OF RELAXATION

These examples illustrate what is perhaps the central idea of cognitive-behavioral relaxation training. Both client and trainer become scientists and artists, actively experimenting and exploring while at the same time constructing relaxation sequences with structure and meaning. The metaphor of scientific inquiry is frequently used to describe the client role in behavior therapy (Bedrosian & Beck, 1980; Guidano & Liotti, 1983; Kelly, 1955; Mahoney, 1974); however, it is somewhat new to view treatment seriously as an art. However, such a conceptualization goes to the heart of what cognitive-behavioral relaxation training is all about. The art of relaxation is to make exercises meaningful and interesting, and thereby enhance a client's motivation to practice. It is to skillfully weave together complex exercise combinations, facilitating their retention. It is to transform relaxation from a mechanical health chore to a reminder of personal beliefs, values, and commitments conducive to increased calm. In broadest terms, the art of relaxation is to help a client discover a source of inner calm and serenity in the midst of life's activities.

APPENDIX A

The Lessons of History

We have completed our presentation of cognitive-behavioral relaxation training and are ready to step back and take a broader look at the evolution of procedures popular today. This history has important lessons to teach.

Relaxation training is as old as civilization itself. Over the centuries ancient procedures have emerged and reemerged from magic, religion, and then science. Antecedents to contemporary relaxation first appeared nearly 5000 years ago in magical rituals of Egypt and India. At this time, priests and holy men used a variety of eye fixation exercises and verbal chants to invoke assistance from the gods and spirits or induce curative sleep (Edmonston, 1986). Similar rituals persisted through Greek and Roman times, the Celtic and Christian domination of Europe, and up to the eighteenth century. By the eighteenth century a burgeoning catalog of rituals had evolved. Their theoretical base often considered the notion of a vital spirit, flux, or magnetic fluid that could flow from one person to another. Techniques included laying on of hands, focusing of attention, use of chants and incantations, and even magnets for directing the flow of vital spirit. Odd as these notions may seem to contemporary minds, they form the direct precursor to much of relaxation as it is known today. We begin with the first secular approaches to relaxation: authoritarian hypnosis, yoga, and meditation.

AUTHORITARIAN HYPNOSIS

To understand the beginnings of hypnosis, we need to begin with Father Johann Joseph Gassner, a Catholic priest who earned notoriety in the

1700s by performing exorcisms in Switzerland and Germany (Edmonston, 1986; Hilgard & Hilgard, 1975). After receiving a ritual incantation, the Father's patients would display convulsions and spasms signaling the release of evil spirits and unwanted symptoms. Many opposed Gassner, this being the Age of Enlightenment, and in 1775 local authorities appointed a commission to investigate his magical cures. At the commission's invitation a prominent Austrian physician, Franz Anton Mesmer, proceeded to demonstrate that Gassner's convulsions and cures could be produced by what appeared to be naturalistic methods. Gassner was then sent off as a priest to a small community and eventually the Pope himself placed limits on the practice of exorcism. Mesmer in turn proceeded to develop a large and lucrative practice.

Mesmer's story is one worth telling in detail. It not only depicts the introduction of the first formal secular approach to relaxation, indeed the first relaxation fad, but can serve as a parable of the rocky and often confused relationship among scientific, religious, and magical approaches to understanding relaxation. As we have seen, religious and magical traditions can for some provide a rich store of metaphors for enriching relaxation practice. However, such traditions also have potential for considerable harm and can be the source of dogmatic and counterproductive adherence to pseudoscientific attitudes.

Mesmer's naturalistic approach to "exorcism" was of course mesmerism, or animal magnetism, and was a direct precursor to contemporary hypnosis (Edmonston, 1986; Hilgard & Hilgard, 1975). Mesmer believed that living bodies possess a magnetic fluid which, when out of balance, contributes to misery and illness. In addition, transfer of "fluid" to patients in distress would initially induce a "crisis," or convulsions, and eventually bring fluids into balance, curing patients of a variety of maladies.

Mesmer's method seemed scientific for the times. Instead of relying on supernatural entities, he would have patients sit around a *baquet*—a tub filled with water and iron filings (substances frequently used in supernatural rituals)—and hold onto iron rods through which animal magnetism might reach their bodies. Mesmer himself would appear in elegant violet silk robes and assist. The mirrored room was darkened and silenced, except for the occasional strains of a harpsichord or the newly-invented harmonium. Using an iron staff, he stroked patients, gazed into their eyes, until the transfer of magnetic fluid was complete. Patients often cried hysterically, fell into convulsions, and collapsed into sleep. Each was then removed into a silk padded *chambre des crises* to recuperate.

Although Mesmer produced many spectacular cures, he fell in disfavor with the French authorities (who were perhaps not so much concerned with rumors of amorous goings on in Mesmer's silken chambers as with reports of possible political indoctrination). In 1784, nearly a decade after Gassner, it was Mesmer's turn to be investigated. At this time the French Academy of Medicine appointed a special commission of inquiry consisting of none less than Benjamin Franklin, the American Ambassador to France, Lavoisier, the noted chemist, and with some irony, Guillotine, inventor of the "merciful" machine of execution that bears his name. The commission's conclusion represented essentially the first cognitive-behavioral appraisal of a secular relaxation procedure: Mesmerism was not the product of magnetism, animal or otherwise, but of mere imagination. Although Mesmer was not beheaded, he left France disgraced, ostracized and isolated. Mesmerism, however, spread to other parts of the world and in America may well have contributed to the development of the Religious movement known as Christian Science. The final irony is that imagination, the discounting argument of Franklin, Lavoisier, and Guillotine, is today central to many theories of hypnosis and relaxation.

Strange and magical as Mesmer's techniques and theories may seem to us, they do represent an important transition. Although his techniques were not unlike those used in medieval demonic exorcisms, his theory was clearly secular. Animal magnetism was presumably a natural phenomenon, quite apart from the gods, spirits, and demons of antiquity.

Although Mesmer's theories were quickly discarded, a number of physicians were impressed by his results. Two English surgeons, Elliotson and Esdaile, reported on numerous dramatic surgeries done under hypnosis without anesthetic. Another influential English physician, James Braid, theorized that deliberately fixing attention on a single, continuous, monotonous stimulus, evokes a special nervous sleep or stupor, a condition he termed *neuro-hypnotism,* or hypnosis.

By the time of Braid, hypnosis was coming of age. Consistencies in nineteenth century induction procedures were beginning to emerge, forming what can be called the authoritarian approach to hypnosis. Techniques frequently involved eye fixation and sleep suggestion. Most important, the hypnotist took the role of an authoritarian teacher or physician, directly presenting or commanding suggestions (even to the point of ordering "Sleep!"). The hypnotized subject took a passive and compliant role. A set of responses came to define hypnotic suggestion, including age regression, amnesia, anesthesia, distortions in body image, hallucination, immobilization and catalepsy, (inability to open the eyes or jaws, separate closed hands, remove hands from the forehead, etc.), involuntary movement (swaying, swallowing, etc.), and posthypnotic suggestion (Edmonston, 1986).

Hypnosis was the first approach to secular relaxation to appear in the West. Although debates continue regarding the relationship between hypnosis and relaxation (Edmonston, 1981; Sarbin & Slagle, 1979), it is safe to say that since its onset, the induction of relaxation has almost always been one of the objectives of relaxation, and relaxation has frequently been a tool used in hypnotic induction.

YOGA AND MEDITATION

The early origins of yoga and meditation can also be traced to eye fixation exercises and verbal chants as early as 3000 B.C. However, unlike hypnosis, the evolution of relaxation in India, China, and eventually Japan, was more closely tied to the development of the prevailing religious traditions, specifically Hinduism and Buddhism. By the second century BC, a diverse assortment of yoga, breathing, and meditation concentration exercises, were codified in the yoga aphorisms of Patanjali (Eliade, 1969; Prabhavananda, 1963). Their goals, although often resembling the magical healing and religious exercises of the West, emphasized the cultivation of a meditative state of mind conducive to spiritual insight. Patanjali's path outlined eight key steps, which included various initial ascetic practices, yoga postures and breathing exercises, and finally meditation. The easiest of meditative practices involved withdrawing the senses from the troubling and distracting influence of external stimuli, memories, and so on, and concentrating on a single point. Through the centuries, numerous divisions of Hindu thinking appeared, some emphasizing devotion to a Christian-like God and others an impersonal absolute. This latter position, associated with the ancient philosoher Shankara, was to eventually to form the basis of most Western forms of Hinduism and yoga.

Around 600 B.C. Buddhism emerged as an offshoot of Hinduism that emphasized meditation over yoga postures (Conze, 1959; Layman, 1976). In addition, Buddha taught that existence is permeated with suffering caused by selfish thought. Selfish thought could be destroyed by following an "eightfold path" of right motivation and conduct eventually culminating in meditation. In the sixth century Buddhism was carried to China and appeared 600 years later in Japan as Zen. Zen emphasizes meditation over theological and philosophical inquiry, prayer, and the occult and magic. Most popular techniques include counting breaths, meditation upon a *koan* (a type a riddle), and *shikantaza*, or "just sitting."

Although Oriental religious thinking was introduced to the West about a century after Mesmer by the somewhat mystical Theosophical Society, secularized yoga and meditation have somewhat later roots. At the 1893 Chicago World Columbian Exposition, the World Parliament of Religions attracted considerable attention. Representatives from religions around the world were invited to participate in an elaborate display of religious consmopolitanism. It is at the Chicago conference that a brightly robed Swami Vivekananda and Abbot Soyen Shaku formally and ceremoniously introduced Hinduism and Zen Buddhism to the American continent (Marty, 1986). The version of Hinduism introduced was a somewhat secularized rendition of the thinking of Shankara. Its message emphasized the fundamental unity of all religions and meditative experience as the prime source of religious knowledge. Most important, it permitted viewing religious insight as valid only if it did not contradict reason or science (Prabhavananda, 1968), a position which left little room for magic and the occult. Yoga and meditative practices, essentially those summarized by Patanjali, had as their primary goal the development of concentration and clearing of the mind. Westernized Zen Buddhism had a similar, cognitive and experiential emphasis. Magic, occult, the supernatural, and even philosophical inquiry were deemphasized in place of psychological/existential insight and the simple practice of meditation. These somewhat secularized versions of Hinduism and Buddhism slowly attracted interest, notably that of William James (1902). Zen and Vedanta Hindu societies were established in major American cities, gradually to form the basis of hundreds of meditation and yoga programs.

CONTEMPORARY SYSTEMS OF RELAXATION

Autogenic Training

Autogenic training has its roots in hypnosis. During the years 1890 and 1900, Berlin neurophysiologist Oskar Vogt developed an approach to hypnosis that is an antecedent of contemporary nonauthoritarian approaches. Instead of directly commanding suggestions, he gently hinted at what we wanted a patient to do or perceive. His wish was not to disturb the patient's freedom of will. In addition, he introduced a step-by-step approach, the "fraction method," in which a patient would be hypnotized for a few minutes, and awoken. The effects of each brief hypnosis would be ascertained and used to adjust subsequent suggestions (Loewenfeld, 1901). Finally, Vogt made the important observation that a number of his hypnosis patients were able to induce their own hypnotic-like states (Schultz & Luthe, 1959) and that these states, when evoked a few times a day, appeared to have therapeutic value.

Around the same time a dermatologist, Johannes Schultz, shifted to neurology and psychiatry and began practicing hypnosis. Schultz made use of the notion that thinking of sensations related to relaxation can often evoke relaxation. In the 1920s and 1930s he introduced autogenic training, a relaxation-based system of therapy that minimized dependency on a therapist (Schultz, 1932). During the course of his career, Schultz published more than 400 articles and several books. His system became widely known in Europe and was introduced in the Western hemisphere by Wolfgang Luthe (1965).

Traditional autogenic training is a highly structured sequential program (Luthe, 1969–1973). It begins with six standard exercises that involve mentally repeating verbal formulae targeted to heaviness, warmth, cardiac regulation, respiration, abdominal warmth, and cooling of the forehead. Emphasis is placed on "passive volition," that is, repeating formulae passively, while maintaining complete indifference about the result. Once the standard exercises are mastered, a variety of special exercises may be introduced. Organ-specific formulae tailor the standard exercises to the particular needs of the patient. For example, a backache patient may use the phrase "My back is warm," a headache patient, "My forehead is cool," and so on. Intentional formulae are phrases targeted to behavioral change objectives ("I will study more, drink less").

Next a series of seven "meditative," or imagery, exercises are presented. Patients begin by attending to color sensations that spontaneously occur with eyes closed in relaxation. Then, the colors that appear most frequently are attended to until they can be produced and modulated on demand. The patient proceeds to visualize simple concrete objects, abstract constructs (truth, justice, and friendship), emotional states, and other people. Eventually, exercises are directed toward seeking "answers from the unconscious," i.e., asking questions ("What is the source of my rage") and passively waiting for a spontaneous answer to emerge.

Today, autogenic training is frequently shortened to simply warmth and heaviness formulae. In addition, abbreviated variations have emerged with highly specific suggestions targeted, for example, to individual cancer tumors, the immune system, and so on (Simonton, Matthews-Simonton, & Creighton, 1978). Such variations are at times presented as having nearly magical healing potential and have attracted a modest cult of advocates.

Nonauthoritarian Hypnosis

Since the time of Vogt, the nature of hypnosis gradually became less authoritarian and more "client-centered." Initially, less emphasis was placed on the external hypnotizing influence of "electricity" or "fluids," and more on the subject's own imagination. The hypnotist would spend more time explaining hypnosis to the subject and developing rapport. Eventually, the hypnotist and subject became collaborators in a joint venture, with the hypnotist taking more of a role of guide than authoritarian director.

A typical contemporary nonauthoritarian hypnotic induction (Wolberg, 1948) might begin with monotonous patter suggesting drowsiness and relaxation while directing attention to a restricted stimulus or set of sensations. As the subject begins to relax, certain physiological changes may occur, some associated with relaxation (spontaneous muscle jerks), others with continually maintaining attention (watery eyes). These may be interpreted or suggested to the subject as initial signs of hypnotic trance. After a set of suggestions intended to deepen drowsiness and relaxation, a graduated series of hypnotic tasks are presented, each requiring and contributing to a greater degree of hypnotic responsivitiy ("eyelids so heavy they cannot be opened . . . arms and legs so heavy they cannot be lifted . . . hands clasped together so tightly they cannot be opened"). Eventually, the subject is ready for such standard hypnotic suggestions as hand numbness, age regression, hallucination, and posthypnotic suggestion.

Two prolific and influential figures, Milton Erickson and Theodore Xenophon Barber, illustrate the diversity of recent versions of nonauthoritarian hypnosis. Erickson's approach has become immensely popular, and indeed is becoming something of a cult. There is no one "Ericksonian" induction system, but a highly individualized assortment of techniques loosely based on psychodynamic principles (Erickson, Rossi, & Rossi, 1976). This repertoire includes use of *confusion, diversion, and double binds* (suggesting the opposite of what is intended, presenting conflicting messages), *indirect induction* (nonverbal communication, introducing suggestions by means of indirect metaphor), and use of *naturalistic techniques* (weaving clients existing symptoms, images, and experiences into the induction). Although Erickson did not develop a formal theory, his techniques rely heavily on notions of the "unconscious." He would direct suggestions, either directly or indirectly, to the presumed hidden or unconscious side of a patient. To this end, techniques such as confusion, diversion, double bind, and indirect induction were designed to bypass, exhaust, or divert goal-directed analytic thinking. However, Erickson did not present himself in the traditional psychoanalytic doctor–patient role. Each induction was molded and modified to fit what the patient was experiencing. Most important, hypnosis was a cooperative venture, with the hypnotist serving as a guide.

In contrast to Erickson, Theodore Xenophon Barber comes from a behavioral tradition that avoids the term "hypnosis" and "trance" as unnecessary and potentially misleading constructs. His preference is to focus on those conditions conducive to evoking "hypnotic" responses, specifically "task-motivational instructions" targeted to changing attitudes, motivations, and expectancies (Barber, 1984). Barber's approach includes inducing a state of deep relaxation, defining the situation as "hypnosis," noting that the suggestions are "easy" and can be "passed" by most subjects, reducing critical and analytic thinking, and vividly imagining what is described in suggestions. Once appropriate conditions are established, the hypnotist can proceed to introduce typical hypnotic task suggestions.

A recent innovation, which Barber (1984) calls "philosophical hypnosis," strives to nurture a level of "equanimity or peace of mind" that goes beyond muscle relaxation. His suggestions incorporate a set of four philosophical principles for coping with the difficulties of life:

1. For every human being, life has its problems. In order to live happily, one must be able to accept this as an inevitable fact.
2. Current problems should be faced by calmly asking "Can I change things for the better, and, if so, how?"
3. One must also realize that many things simply cannot be changed.
4. When dealing with the difficulties of life, it is often helpful to (a) think ahead and calmly prepare for future problems; (b) become more accepting, nonjudgmental, compassionate, and loving; (c) emphasize the positive aspects of ourselves and others; and (d) be a model for and help others.

Although Barber's specific "philosophy of life" may not be appropriate for everyone, his approach represents a blend of cognitive-behavior modification and hypnosis. As such it anticipates cognitive-behavioral relaxation training.

Progressive Relaxation

Progressive relaxation is perhaps the most widely used approach to relaxation in America. For years it has dominated textbooks and relaxation research and, until recently, it was not unusual to see the term "progressive relaxation" used interchangeably with relaxation itself.

Progressive relaxation was developed in the early twentieth century by physician and psychologist Edmund Jacobson. It is a system that owes much to the prevailing interest of academic psychology in perception and physiology and little to hypnosis, yoga, or meditation. Jacobson began his work on relaxation as a doctoral student at Harvard in 1907, prompted in part by his desire to cure his own insomnia (Jacobson, 1938). In 1926 he joined the Department of Physiology at the University of Chicago and conducted research on the knee-jerk reflex. Jacobson gradually developed a private practice, often making use of relaxation procedures. At first, he used reductions in the knee-jerk reflex as a sign of relaxation and a tool for refining relaxation techniques. Later, he enlisted the aid of scientists at Bell Telephone Laboratory and invented the integrated neurovoltmeter, essentially an electromyograph capable of measuring tension-related action potentials from muscle groups and nerves. With this equipment, Jacobson developed and practiced his method of progressive relaxation for over five decades.

Jacobson's approach (1929, 1938) involved training subjects to detect and recognize increasingly subtle levels of muscle tension and remain relaxed throughout the day. In each session a subject would generate the smallest amount of tension possible, and then let go. Care was taken to avoid suggestive patter that might introduce confounding hypnotic effects (ironically, some hypnosis scholars consider Jacobson's approach to be a form of hypnosis; Edmonston, 1986). Subjects would be taught to relax two or three muscle groups per session, eventually covering 50 groups for the entire body. Training required 50 or more sessions that could last from 3 to 6 months to over a year.

Jacobson's method was cumbersome and not widely used. In 1958 Joseph Wolpe (1958) introduced the first of several streamlined versions of progressive relaxation. Earlier, Wolpe had found that a conditioned fear reaction in cats could be eliminated by evoking a response incompatible with fear concurrently with a feared stimulus. Progressive relaxation presented a convenient "reciprocal inhibitor" and became a part of Wolpe's well-known desensitization treatments. Indeed, the two became so closely identified that occasionally researchers would erroneously use "progressive relaxation" and "desensitization" interchangeably.

Today's popular streamlined approaches of Wolpe and others place greater emphasis on creating a considerable level of relaxation in the first session by effortfully generating and releasing tension. Often up to 16 muscle groups, rather than one to three, are targeted. As training progresses, muscle groups are combined until eventually the subject can simply detect and relax tension without first overtly creating tension. In the most abbreviated format, termed conditioned relaxation (Paul, 1966) and cue-controlled relaxation (Russell & Matthews, 1975), a subject covertly thinks a relaxing cue word, such as "relaxed" or "calm," after practicing progressive relaxation. In time, the cue itself is sufficient to evoke relaxation.

Lamaze and Breathing Exercises

Although breathing plays an important part in virtually every system of relaxation used by health professionals, it has not emerged in itself as a prominent approach, nor has it attracted much research. However, the popular Lamaze approach to childbirth does rely heavily on breathing manipulations.

Lamaze techniques evolved from late eighteenth century Russian and European attempts to reduce the pain of childbirth through hypnosis. However, hypnosis was soon replaced by procedures derived from three Pavlovian ideas (Wideman & Singer, 1984). First, the pain of childbirth is partly the result of classical conditioning. Second, the practice of breathing exercises in labor creates a focus of "cerebral activation" so strong that other areas of the cortex are inhibited from responding to pain stimuli. Third, verbal stimuli can be conditioned to pain inhibitors. Put simply, verbal commands and uterine contractions, when paired with breathing exercises, are eventually sufficient to trigger inhibitory, pain-reducing processes in the cortex. It should be noted that this is essentially the same procedure used by Wolpe (1958) to treat phobias, the main difference being that Wolpe used progressive relaxation rather than breathing as a reciprocal inhibitor.

The Soviet Union adopted the Pavlovian-based approach in 1951 as the official method of childbirth. Soon after, a French obstetrician, Lamaze, observed the procedures and incorporated many into what is known today as the Lamaze method. Today, Lamaze procedures are widely applied in hospitals in the United States (Wideman and Singer, 1984). Although the specific methods bear close resemblance to auto-genic training, progressive relaxation, and classical desensitization, and are based in a large part on psychological theory, they have attracted little research or interest as anything other than an approach to "natural childbirth."

Most Lamaze classes involve instruction in the anatomy and physiology of gestation and parturition, respiration techniques, progressive relaxation, attentional diversion (focusing on sucking on hard candies; attending to a spot on the wall, etc.), concentrating on relaxing words or phrases while practicing relaxation, and training of a labor coach (Wideman & Singer 1984). Respiration exercises include the use of rapid breathing during the second stage of labor and panting during delivery. Women are trained to ensure a balanced level of carbon dioxide and oxygen by controlling breathing. Additional special breathing exercises are taught at each stage.

No discussion of breathing would be complete without noting other breathing exercises little known to most health professionals. First, many meditative techniques (to be discussed later) incorporate breathing as a meditative focus (Kapleau, 1965; Benson, 1975). However, Hindu yoga tradition has incorporated the greatest diversity of breathing exercises, numbering in the hundreds (Iyengar, 1981). An entire yoga literature exists on breathing alone, and there are Hindu monasteries devoted exclusively to breathing exercises (Rama, Ballentine, & Hymes, 1979).

The ancient yoga tradition dedicated to breathing exercises is called *pranayama*. Prana is the Sanskrit term for life energy as well as breath. In pranayama it is believed that mastering breath enables one to experience and even control life energy. Exercises range from those that are relatively passive, including attending to the flow of breath and breathing alternately through each nostril, to actively panting, pulling in abdominal muscles (to constrict the diaphragm), and bowing and stretching. Some exercises are extremely difficult and require years of mastery. In fact practitioners of pranayama can be likened to both lifelong athletes and musicians, achieving considerable control over physiological breathing processes while learning to appreciate the subtleties of breathing, almost as an art form. At the highest level of abstraction, pranayama is also a spiritual discipline, a vehicle for coming in touch with the absolute.

Given the absence of research on breathing exercises, it is not surprising that there is no consensus as to what constitutes relaxed breathing. Most yoga exercises emphasize an even, rhythmical pattern of inhalation and exhalation as well as increased use of the diaphragm. Other exercises are directed toward either increasing or decreasing breathing pace, volume, and length of pauses (Smith, 1989). It is clear that tension can affect breathing in many ways and that there is no single way breathing can enhance relaxation.

Imagery

Imagery has been diversely applied as an approach to relaxation, either alone or as part of another procedure. Images often form an important part of hypnotic induction and the production of hallucination is a frequently suggested hypnotic response. We have noted that the advanced exercises of autogenic training incorporate a graduated series of simple and complex images. Meditative traditions are rich sources of imagery exercises, with focal stimuli that can be as complex as a circular patterned mandala or simple as a candle flame. Imagery exercises are frequently a part of psychotherapy, and range from the association techniques of Freud and Jung to desensitization and covert modeling techniques of behavior therapy. Finally, visualization often plays an important part in various quasi-scientific treatment and self-improvement programs that exist on the fringe of psychology.

Given its pervasiveness throughout time, perhaps the best way of understanding imagery is to catalog its diversity. All forms of imagery involve producing a covert or mental representation of external stimuli. As a relaxation tool, most techniques include fantasy and daydream that differ primarily in content. Content dimensions include: simplicity, degree of future and goal orientation, rationality, and appropriateness of theme (Singer, 1975; Crits-Cristoph & Singer, 1981). Specific images can include attending to a simple point of light, relaxing in nature setting, recalling a childhood triumph, realistically rehearsing coping with a future stressor, or even engaging in fantasy unconstrained by reality.

Imagery can also be classified according to the modality of content, that is, visual, verbal, auditory, olfactory, tactile, gustatory, or kinesthetic. Typically, content is visual, with other sense modalities introduced as elaborations. Verbal imagery is somewhat less widely used, the most prominent example being autogenic "formulae," phrases which one passively repeats ("My hands are warm and heavy."). In addition, cognitive-behavior therapy (Beck, 1976; Ellis & Grieger, 1977; Meichenbaum, 1977) employs a wide range of covert verbalizations that involve mentally rehearsing self-statements and dialogues designed to be adaptive or rational. Such verbalizations become imagery when they incorporate concrete representations of oneself and the environment (e.g., a test-anxious student taking an exam might think, "I slowly pick up my pencil and answer one question at a time; many people taking this exam are as nervous as I am."). Finally, an undetermined, but possibly large, number of people relax by covertly reciting a variety of personally meaningful poems, stories, songs, and prayers. It is surprising that such verbal imagery has rarely been considered in the scientific study of relaxation.

Imagery can be also classified according to its goal. Uncovering exercises involve exploring feelings and conflicts not immediately accessible to verbal report. Common examples include free association (Freud, 1913), active imagination (Jung, 1976), and "focusing" (Gendlin, 1981). In contrast, creativity exercises are more likely to have a positive focus (Masters & Houston, 1972; Samuels & Samuels, 1975). It is interesting to note the close connection between uncovering and creativity exercises; Freud, often seen as one of the originators of association techniques, acknowledged that the germ of his idea came from a creative writing exercise he encountered in childhood (Freud, 1920). Gendlin, one of the most recent proponents of association techniques in therapy, suggests applying them to other purposes, such as enhancing creativity, dream interpretation, and so on (Gendlin, 1981).

Rarely do texts on relaxation include uncovering or creativity techniques. But from the standpoint of their originators, relaxation is clearly a presumed byproduct of such procedures, that is, as a conflict is uncovered, its potential for creating tension is diminished. Furthermore, when imagery is used as a creativity exercise, rather than as a tool for probing sources of distress, the approach becomes virtually indistinguishable from fantasy and daydream, save for predetermined creative goal. As a potential imagery theme, there is no reason to discount creative exploration over the commonly applied reminiscence or nature scenes.

Verbal Meditation

We began our historical exploration with a discussion of the emergence of secular relaxation. It is ironic that this is where we end. Meditation represents perhaps the only recent approach to relaxation where seasoned scientists and health professionals not only approached, but embraced a system with blatant magical and religious components.

In 1959, an Indian guru, Maharishi Mahesh Yogi, arrived in the United States with no less a goal than to start a new worldwide movement based on a technique, transcendental meditation (TM). His technique was actually a form of Hindu meditation derived from exercises suggested by Patanjali minus the preparation exercises. Specifically, one quietly and passively attends to a "mantra," a "meaningless" neutral sound or Sanskrit word. At first the Maharishi attracted little attention. However, with a little help from the Beatles and the emerging interest in experimenting with altered states of consciousness (Stone, 1976; Tart, 1969), TM attracted about 35,000 practitioners by 1970 (Bloomfield, Cain, & Jaffe, 1975).

Transcendental meditation received a considerable boost from three influential studies. Wallace and his colleagues (Wallace, 1970; Wallace & Benson, 1972; Wallace, Benson, & Wilson, 1971) examined the physiological state displayed by TM meditators during, before, and after meditation. During meditation, subjects show what appears to be the opposite of the fight-or-flight or defense alarm reaction described by Cannon (1932). The TM organization seized upon this finding as a demonstration of no less than a "fourth major state of consciousness," the others being wakefulness, sleep with dreaming, and sleep without dreaming. Furthermore, this state was claimed to be a unique and automatic effect of meditation.

Such studies attracted considerable interest and did much to foster TM's image as a secular technique. Soon, more scholarly studies appeared on TM than any other form of meditation and by 1975 the technique had been taught to one million people (Orme-Johnson & Farrow, 1977). Indeed, 1975 was proclaimed by the Maharishi as no less than "The Dawn of the Age of Enlightenment" (Orme-Johnson & Farrow, 1977). Today, a large number of behavior therapy and clinical psychology texts place TM on equal footing with progressive relaxation and autogenic training as a serious, secular treatment option. More often than not, TM is described as synonymous with meditation itself.

In spite of its acceptance, TM can only be described as a pseudoscientific cult. Introductory lectures make frequent and lavish use of research, overstating supportive findings and ignoring the negative. TM has held large group meditations, in its gold domed meditation hall at Maharishi International University in Iowa, to influence weather patterns, world events (as far away as in Lebanon), and the stock market. Furthermore, by practicing an advanced version of TM, it is claimed one can acquire dramatic psychic powers, such as seeing through walls, looking into the future, becoming invisible, and levitating. Even more dramatically, TM has claimed scientific proof that its technique can increase intelligence, productivity, and creativity; erase mental illness, crime, drug abuse, and poverty; prolong life, and so on (Orme-Johnson & Farrow, 1977). The cultic flavor of TM was revealed vividly in a full-page advertisement in *Time* magazine (September 5, 1983, p. 2) proclaiming the formation of a TM-based "world government" willing (and guaranteeing) "to solve the problems of any government regardless of the magnitude and nature of the problem—political, economic, social, or religious; and irrespective of its system—capitalism, communism, socialism, democracy, or dictatorship." Beside such claims, the exorcisms and magical incantations prior to Mesmer seem pale indeed.

A number of scientists recognized TM's cultic aspects and proceeded to develop meditations of their own. Benson, who initially collaborated with Wallace, eventually became dissatisfied and developed a "relaxation response" technique. This approach has been widely and erroneously presented in clinical texts as "noncultic TM"; it is in fact a modified Zen exercise involving attending to the word "one" on every exhalation. Clinical psychologist Patricia Carrington also broke away from TM and developed a detailed alternative that carefully includes all procedural aspects of TM, and avoids cultic aspects. Other, similar approaches to meditation have emerged.

Today, primarily due to the influence of TM, textbooks present a consistently one-sided version of meditation. First, unlike traditional Zen and Hindu approaches, meditation is presented without preparatory exercises. Second, Western meditation is almost exclusively verbal. Focal stimuli are either mantras, the word "one," or simple, pleasing, relaxing words.

RELAXATION TODAY

What does the history of relaxation tell us? First, from Mesmer to TM's Maharishi, proponents of relaxation have often flirted with the fringes of cult and pseudoscience. It is all too easy to be a relaxation magician or priest, promoting a private vision of God, the unconscious, internal healing potentials, and so on.

Second, the evolution of relaxation procedures (other than biofeedback) has remained essentially static for decades. Changes that have occurred, for example, streamlining progressive relaxation, introducing nonauthoritarian suggestions in hypnosis, relying exclusively on "warmth/heaviness" suggestions in autogenic training, and eliminating stretching and breathing preparation in verbal meditation, represent relatively minor alterations or simplifications of basic approaches.

However, our history makes one point especially clear. The world of relaxation is a chaotic profusion of approaches—authoritarian hypnosis, yoga, meditation, nonauthoritarian hypnosis, autogenic training, progressive relaxation, Lamaze, imagery, and verbal meditation. Each approach in turn has countless variations. Such a state of affairs might tempt one to retreat into the secure and narrow-minded belief that a specific favored system represents all there is to know of relaxation. However, if this book has one overall goal, it is to challenge such thinking. There is much to discover about relaxation. It is a world waiting to be explored.

APPENDIX B

The Basic Protocol: Rules for Making a Relaxation Script

A thorough way to set up a client relaxation program is to make a detailed script of exercise instructions. This script can then be tape recorded, directly read to the practitioner, or used as an informal outline for personal practice. Even if a script is not formally used in training or practice, writing one can be a useful exercise for defining the content and direction of an exercise sequence and gaining practice in employing cognitive-behavioral relaxation principles.

The first step is to teach a variety of relaxation procedures. I recommend selecting exercises that are "pure" representations of at least five of the nine approaches on the relaxation hierarchy. Written and audiocassette instructions are available elsewhere (Smith, 1986a, 1989).

Traditional relaxation training often ends after exercises are taught. However, this is where cognitive-behavioral relaxation training begins. In assigning relaxation to a client, three levels of individualization are possible, depending on client motivation and available time. The easiest strategy is to simply assign whatever general approach the client prefers. For example, if, after trying sets of isometric squeeze, yogaform stretching, breathing, imagery, and meditation exercises, the client prefers breathing, then that is what the client continues practicing. A somewhat more individualized strategy is to combine preferred exercises from several approaches into a relaxation sequence. For example, a client may prefer to begin with four isometric squeeze exercises, perhaps the shoulder, neck, face, and back squeeze, proceed to imagery, and end with meditation. The most individualized approach is to construct a relaxation script. Here, the client and therapist become scientists and artists, carefully selecting exercises that work best and constructing a sequence with coherence and integrity. It is worth reiterating that a well-made script can make a potentially dry and mechanical exercise enjoyable and interesting. Because each element fits in a meaningful way, a sequence is more likely to be remembered and practiced in its entirety. Most important, a set of exercises should ultimately serve as a reminder and expression of those skills, beliefs, values, and commitments that can extend the promise of relaxation to all of life.

WRITING A SCRIPT

This protocol describes three steps in writing a relaxation script: (a) selecting a relaxation goal, unifying idea, and exercise sequence; (b) making elaborations; and (c) adding refinements. These steps can be used as a formal guide for constructing a relaxation program or as a source of ideas for enhancing a program that has already been established (Table B.1).

Constructing a comprehensive relaxation program from scratch can involve many levels of revision. The trainer first writes down a set of basic instructions, and adds to them again and again. This can get complicated unless one has a system. I recommend using a pack of

TABLE B.1 Summary of Steps in Writing a Relaxation Script

Selection
1. Relaxation goal
2. Unifying idea
3. Specific exercises
4. Sequence

Elaboration
1. Incorporation of unifying idea
2. Imagery details
3. Somatic sensations, skills, and structures
4. Deepening strategies (optional)
5. Sequence coherence

Refinement
1. Anticipations of setback
2. Relaxation reinforcements
3. Pauses and silences
4. Termination segment

index cards (3″ × 5″) and two colored pens. One writes down concrete exercise instructions (for example, "Take in a deep breath . . . shrug your shoulders . . .") in one color, making sure to put no more than one statement on each card. Then, refinements and elaborations ("Let yourself relax more and more completely . . .") are placed on additional cards using a different color of ink. Once again, no more than one statement should be placed on each card. When this is finished, the trainer will have two stacks of cards, one with basic instructions, and one with refinements and elaborations. Refinement and elaboration cards can be placed in appropriate places in the instruction deck. When finished, the trainer can copy the completed set of cards on a single script.

In the following example, a script is constructed for a hypothetical client, Sue. To save space, some details and repetitions have been omitted. Each revision or addition is highlighted in **boldface** type.

Selection

Relaxation Goal

The client must first decide why he or she wants to relax. Possible goals include: managing stress, combating insomnia, relaxing at the end of the day, waking up refreshed in the morning, enhancing creativity and productivity, and self-exploration and growth. Sue's goal is "daily relaxation for self-expression and growth."

ENTER CLIENT'S RELAXATION GOAL.

Unifying Idea

An exercise sequence acquires structure and meaning from a unifying idea, a statement of a sequence's overjustification, what it is all about. Once a unifying idea is selected, it should be woven into exercise components (instructions for doing this will be presented in a later section). There are five possible types of unifying ideas:

1. Exercise Rationale (explanation why it works)
2. Exercise Goal
3. Affirmation of a Personal Relaxation Philosophy
4. Relaxation Metaphor or Image
5. Relaxation Story

Often, a unifying idea is little more than the rationale provided by the relaxation trainer. For example, a practitioner of isometric squeeze relaxation would probably think of each exercise enhancing ability to discriminate and let go of tension.

A relaxation goal can be simply the pragmatic reason for practicing relaxation, for example: "stress release," "combating insomnia," "waking up refreshed for the day," "preparing for work," or even "prayer" or "communing with nature." A goal can also be artistic expression. Here, constructing or practicing an exercise becomes a special and somewhat unusual art form, one with the dual goals of creating a thing of beauty and evoking relaxation. Put differently, techniques of relaxation become an expressive medium, analogous to the words of a poet, the paints of an artist, or the dance steps of a choreographer.

Unifying ideas can be affirmations of personal relaxation philosophies, or "structures," for example, "Live in the present moment," "God's will be done," "Let go of that which can not be changed," or "Trust the powers within you."

Metaphors or symbolic representations of relaxation can form the basis of a unifying idea. The theme of a *peaceful woods* might symbolize many aspects of a relaxation sequence. For example, a gentle breeze might symbolize breathing exercises; trees slowly bowing in the wind, stretching exercises; the sun warming the leaves, somatic "warmth and heaviness"; and the silence of approaching evening, a meditative focus of attention. Note how these images are not only peaceful in their own right, but suggestive of specific relaxation exercises. To take an example presented later in this lesson, the theme of *waves crashing on the shore* can symbolize a variety of exercises. The energy that builds and releases with each crashing wave can suggest the tension-release cycle of isometric squeeze relaxation (or inhalation and exhalation of deep breathing). The dissolving of each wave into the sand can be linked with somatic focusing suggestions of "heaviness, tingling, and dissolving tension." And the quiet wind that flows across the water before the next wave can suggest focused breathing.

A unifying idea can be something of a very simple story or changing metaphor, providing all elements are linked to relaxation exercises, change in a direction of increased relaxation, and end in deeper relaxation. For example, the theme of waves crashing on the shore just mentioned is a bit of a story—a wave builds up, crashes, dissolves into the sand, and a quiet wind blows.

Before concluding this discussion, it is useful to note that unifying ideas can be put in the client's own words, or embodied in a passage from a song, poem, prayer, or piece of literature the client has found to be particularly peaceful. One can use the entire passage as an introduction to a relaxation sequence or introduce parts of it into each exercise.

We can now return to Sue's script. Sue has selected the image of sitting on the banks of a mountain stream, a metaphor for the philosophy "Live one day at a time, let useless tension be."

ENTER CLIENT'S UNIFYING IDEA HERE.

Specific Exercises

Next, the client needs to select which exercises he or she wants to include in the relaxation program. As few or as many can be chosen, although the examples presented here include a relatively large variety in order to illustrate every protocol step. In addition, it is at this stage that the client selects focal stimuli for mental exercises (somatic focusing suggestions, imagery theme, contemplation and meditation focus). These should reflect the unifying idea. In writing a script, details for all physical exercises should be included at this point (when cards are used, *each line of instruction* should be entered on a different card). Specifics for imagery exercises should be included later.

Sue has selected isometric squeeze relaxation, breathing, imagery, and open focus meditation as her preferred approaches. Her choices are:

Hand squeeze

Arm squeeze

Shoulder squeeze

Back of neck squeeze

Front of neck squeeze

Leg squeeze

Foot squeeze

Deep breathing

Breathing out through lips

Imagery (Theme: "Sitting on the banks of a mountain stream")

Open focus meditation

THE CLIENT SHOULD NOW SELECT EXERCISES TO INCLUDE IN THE RELAXATION PROGRAM.

Sequence

The next step is to decide an exercise practice order consistent with the unifying idea. It is generally best to proceed from active and complex exercises to those that are passive and simple, although variations from this pattern can be effective. It is possible to combine exercises, for example, a hand and arm stretch, or a hand squeeze and hand stretch. We are now ready to examine excerpts from Sue's script. Detailed instructions for selected physical exercises (isometric squeeze relaxation and breathing) are presented, although those imagery have been left for later.

SUE'S SCRIPT: Exercise Selection and Sequence

[ISOMETRIC SQUEEZE]

Make a tight fist with your right hand.

Hold the tension . . .

Attend to the sensations of tension . . .

And let go.

Let the tension flow . . .

Attend to the feelings of relaxation . . .

Tighten up the muscles in your feet and toes . . .

Let the tension build . . .

And let go.

Let the tension dissolve . . .

Compare the feelings of tension and relaxation.

[BREATHING]

Take in a deep breath, filling your lungs completely.

Gently exhale.

Let the air flow out of your lips with every breath.

[IMAGERY: SITTING ON THE BANKS OF A MOUNTAIN STREAM]

[OPEN FOCUS MEDITATION]

THE CLIENT SHOULD NOW INDICATE A PREFERRED ORDER. IF THE CARD SYSTEM IS BEING USED, ONE PHRASE OR SENTENCE OF INSTRUCTION SHOULD BE PLACED ON EACH CARD.

Elaboration

Incorporation of Unifying Idea

Each exercise component should be linked with the unifying idea. This can be achieved by either an introductory statement or specific phrases woven into each exercise component. For example, the following two sequences incorporate the same rationale and goal as a unifying idea, "breathing out tension and settling into calm." The first makes use of a unifying introduction:

> The following sequence involves relaxing by releasing tension with every outgoing breath. Each breathing exercise becomes less vigorous and effortful as tension melts, dissolves, and dissipates. The more tension floats away, the more you begin to settle into a state of inner calm.
>
> Take in a deep breath. Slowly bow over, let go, and exhale . . .
>
> While sitting upright, breathe in deeply and slowly let go and exhale . . .
>
> Let your breathing be effortless and unforced. Simply attend to each incoming and outgoing breath . . .
>
> Quietly sit and attend to the feelings of calm you have achieved.

In the following segment, the unifying idea is woven into each exercise component:

> Take in a deep breath. Slowly bow over, let go, and exhale.
>
> Let tension begin to melt and flow out with your breath . . .
>
> The following exercise is less vigorous. While sitting upright, breathe in deeply and slowly let go and exhale. As you begin to settle into calm, let more and more tension dissolve and float away . . .
>
> Now, let yourself become even more calm. Let your breathing be effortless and unforced. Simply attend to each incoming and outgoing breath. Let yourself settle into a deeper and deeper state of relaxation as any remaining tension begins to dissipate . . .
>
> Quietly attend to the feelings of calm you have achieved.

A unifying idea can be expressed in a simple story or changing metaphor, for example, "a leaf floating down the river," "a bubble rising to the surface of the pond," or "the sun dissolving a block of ice into a puddle of water." Here is an example in which metaphor changes are woven into a sequence of exercises:

Tense and let go. Imagine a bubble is released from the floor of a pond . . .

Quietly attend to your breathing. Let tension flow with every outgoing breath. As breath flows, the bubble slowly rises.

In your mind's eye, simply attend to the bubble as it reaches the surface. It touches the air, and bursts, releasing its tension. Let go of remaining feelings of tension.

Here again is Sue's script. Note how her unifying idea, the metaphor of sitting on the banks of a mountain stream, is repeated in isometric squeeze relaxation and breathing segments.

SUE'S SCRIPT: Unifying Idea

[ISOMETRIC SQUEEZE]
Make a tight fist with your right hand.

Hold the tension . . .

Attend to the sensations of tension . . .

And let go.

Let the tension flow . . .

IMAGINE YOU ARE SITTING ON THE BANKS OF A MOUNTAIN STREAM, YOUR LEGS DANGLING IN THE WATER.

LET TENSION DISSOLVE INTO THE WATER.

Attend to the feelings of relaxation . . .

Tighten up the muscles in your feet and toes . . .

Let the tension build . . .

And let go.

Let the tension dissolve . . .

LET TENSION FLOW INTO THE WATER.

Compare the feelings of tension and relaxation.

[BREATHING]

Take in a deep breath, filling your lungs completely.

Gently exhale.

Let the air flow out of your lips with every breath.

THE ONLY SOUND YOU HEAR IS THE QUIET FLOW OF BREATH AND A QUIET MOUNTAIN STREAM.

[IMAGERY: SITTING ON THE BANKS OF A MOUNTAIN STREAM]

[MEDITATION]

NOW, INCLUDE THE CLIENT'S UNIFYING IDEA. WHEN USING THE CARD SYSTEM PUT EACH PHRASE OR SENTENCE ON A DIFFERENT CARD.

Imagery Details (optional)

If imagery has been chosen to be part of a relaxation script, it can be incorporated as a separate element or as a component of other elements. For example, a single imagery exercise involving a peaceful palm tree might be placed after a series of stretching and breathing exercises, or woven into each stretching and breathing instruction ("As you stretch and breathe, imagine a palm in the wind."). Also note that somatic focusing, thematic imagery and contemplation require the greatest elaboration (often including a rich variety of suggestions for each sense modality). Instructions for meditation can be more abbreviated. Whatever elaborations are made, it is important that they fit the unifying idea selected. Here is Sue's imagery sequence as well as her closing open focus meditation.

SUE'S SCRIPT with Imagery Exercise Elaboration

[IMAGERY: SITTING ON THE BANKS OF MOUNTAIN STREAM]

NOW, QUIETLY ATTEND ONLY TO THE IMAGE OF SITTING ON THE BANKS OF A COOL, REFRESHING MOUNTAIN STREAM.

YOUR FEET GENTLY SWING IN THE COOL, REFRESHING WATER.

TENSION FLOWS DOWN EACH LEG, INTO YOUR TOES, AND IS DISSOLVED AND CARRIED AWAY BY THE WATER.

YOU CAN SEE THE CLEAR, SPARKLING WATER, SMELL ITS CLEAN SPRAY, AND FEEL THE WARM SUN ON YOUR SKIN.

ATTEND WITH ALL OF YOUR SENSES TO THIS BEAUTIFUL, RELAXING MOMENT.

[MEDITATION]

QUIETLY ATTEND TO THE COMING AND GOING OF THE PRESENT MOMENT.

ELABORATE IMAGERY EXERCISES AT THIS POINT. WHEN USING THE CARD SYSTEM, PUT EACH PHRASE OR SENTENCE ON A DIFFERENT CARD.

Somatic Sensations, Skills, and Structures

An exercise sequence can be enhanced by adding phrases that suggest somatic sensations, relaxation skills, and structures. The following words are loosely suggestive of relaxation somatic sensations:

Bathed	High	Sinking
Caressed	Light	Slack
Cool	Limber	Sleepy
Dissolving	Limp	Slow
Drowsy	Liquid	Smooth
Elastic	Loose	Soft
Flexible	Massaged	Supple
Floating	Mellow	Throbbing
Flowing	Melting	Tingling
Heavy	Sedate	Warm

The following words are loosely suggestive of focusing, passivity, and receptivity (note that some of these words also suggest physical relaxation suggestions):

FOCUSING

Absorbed	Conscious	Mindful
Alert	Contemplative	One-pointed
At one	Deep	Pure
Attentive	Distant	Quiet
Awake	Engrossed	Radiant
Aware	Entranced	Silent
Bright	Far Away	Single-minded
Captivated	Fascinated	Still
Centered	Focused	Stimulated
Charmed	Glowing	Transparent
Cleansed	Interested	Undistracted
Clear	Lucid	
Concentrated	Meditative	

PASSIVITY

At ease	Gratified	Patient
Carefree	Indifferent	Pausing
Contented	Laid back	Playful
Detached	Leisurely	Released
Easy	Letting be	Relieved
Escaped	Letting go	Satisfied
Forgetting	Listless	Selfless
Free	Motionless	Settled
Gentle	Passive	Simple

Spontaneous	Unencumbered	Untroubled
Surrendering	Unforced	Unworried
Unbothered	Unhurried	

RECEPTIVITY

Accepting	Immortal	Rejuvenated
Amazed	Infinite	Renewed
Assured	Innocent	Reverent
Awe	Insightful	Safe
Boundless	Inspired	Secure
Childlike	Intuitive	Speechless
Confident	Liberated	Spiritual
Cosmic	Loving	Thankful
Creative	Mysterious	Timeless
Dreamy	Mystical	Touched
Ecstatic	New	Transcendent
Elated	Open	Transformed
Encouraged	Optimistic	Trusting
Enraptured	Prayerful	Unafraid
Eternal	Profound	Wonder
Expansive	Reassured	Wordless
Glorious	Reborn	Worshipful
Hopeful	Receptive	

A relaxation script can be enhanced by introducing phrases that incorporate such somatic sensation and skill-directed words. These should be introduced no more than once every four lines. Some examples might include:

> Let your fingers become more and more warm. *(somatic sensation)*
>
> Let your body feel lighter and lighter. *(somatic sensation)*
>
> You are becoming more centered. *(focusing)*
>
> Your mind is more attentive. *(focusing)*
>
> Practice easily and effortlessly. *(passivity)*
>
> Experience "letting be." *(passivity)*
>
> You feel increasingly open to possibilities. *(receptivity)*
>
> Trust the hidden processes of relaxation. *(receptivity)*

Additional phrases should affirm relaxing beliefs, values, or commitments by noting any relaxing personal philosophies the client may have. These should be introduced no more than once every ten lines. Some examples follow:

My selfish worries are distractions that fog awareness of a deeper reality.

God loves me and has a plan for my life.

The meaning of life becomes more apparent to me in the quiet of relaxation.

My urgent concerns seem less important when seen in broader perspective.

There are more important things than my everyday hassles.

At the deepest level I can feel at peace with myself—I am an OK person.

I choose to live one day at a time and not worry about things that cannot be changed.

I choose to quit creating unnecessary pain and tension for myself by ignoring my true feelings.

God's will be done.

If a poem or passage of literature expresses what relaxation means to the client, select passages can be incorporated into the script.

Deepening Strategies (optional)

A variety of slightly more advanced strategies can be incorporated to further deepen relaxation. One way is to introduce *deepening imagery*, that is, imagery that changes in a direction of increased focus, passivity, and receptivity. Note how the following imagery is initially complex and active, and then becomes more focused, passive, and receptive:

> You are on a quiet beach. As you sit up and look around, you notice the blue water and sky. The sun is directly overhead, its warm rays dissolving tension in your body. You can feel a breeze and hear the soothing waves splash against the shore. As you become more relaxed, you recline on the beach. Your attention narrows to the sky above, and the peaceful clouds floating by. There is nothing you have to think about or do. Simply attend the clouds and nothing else. All sorts of thoughts and images may come to mind, and that's OK. Simply let them come and go, and return your attention to the graceful clouds.

Metaphors can enhance relaxation deepening processes by symbolizing both concrete exercise procedures and abstract cognitive structures. A swaying tree can signify a yoga stretch or the philosophical statement "Flow with the here and now." Crashing ocean waves can signify the exhalation of breath, or a commitment "Let go of that which cannot be changed." Such metaphors are in a sense more abstract than exercises, and more concrete than cognitive structures. Since they exist at an intermediate level of abstraction, they can be used to foster transitions from concrete conceptualizations of relaxation to more encompassing cognitive structures. This is illustrated in the highly truncated sequence that follows:

> Stretch and unstretch your arms . . .
>
> Stretch and unstretch your legs . . .
>
> With each stretch you are like a tree swaying in the wind . . .
>
> Stretch, unstretch, and sway in the wind . . .
>
> A tree sways in the wind, firmly rooted in the earth, yet flowing with the moment.
>
> Remember how you, firmly supported by the ground of life, can flow with the moment.

If more than one general exercise approach is selected, *deepening transitions* can be introduced between each approach. Such transitions reinforce the appraisal that the sequence is not an arbitrary assortment of exercises, but a progression moving into deeper levels of relaxation. Thus, if a trainee has selected both isometric squeeze and yogaform stretching exercises, the transition between both approaches might read:

> We have now completed one approach to relaxation. We will now move on to another set of exercises many find even more deeply satisfying. As we try these exercises, let yourself become more and more fully relaxed.

Another way to enhance relaxation is to introduce a *relaxation countdown*. One starts with any number, usually 5 or 10, and slowly counts back to 0. Each count is associated with deeper levels of relaxation. To do a countdown, first explain the procedure, as illustrated here:

> I will begin to count backwards from 5 to 0. With each count, let yourself become more and more relaxed.

Then start counting. Between each number introduce a few relaxing phrases. Such a countdown can be introduced in isometric squeeze relaxation, breathing, and imagery. For example, an isometric squeeze relaxation countdown would begin at the onset of each "let go" cycle:

Tense up.

And let go.

We begin with 5.

Attend to the sensations of relaxation.

4

Let the tension slowly begin to flow out of your muscles.

3

Notice the difference between tension and relaxation.

2

Let your muscles become more and more fully relaxed.

1

Let go of any feelings of tension you may feel.

And 0.

Countdowns can be woven into virtually any approach to relaxation. For example, in stretching and breathing sequences, they can be incorporated with unstretching and exhalation. Imagery provides the richest opportunity for countdown relaxation. Here the actual content of an image can change to symbolize increased focusing, passivity, and receptivity with each count. This is illustrated by the following image of floating into the clouds:

> You are resting on earth and become so relaxed that you begin to float.
>
> 5
>
> As you let go of your tensions, you become lighter and lighter.
>
> 4
>
> Your mind centers on the peaceful sensations of floating and relaxation.
>
> 3
>
> You float higher and higher. The houses and trees below become smaller and smaller. Your everyday pressures and concerns seem so distant.
>
> 2
>
> As you approach the peaceful soft clouds, your mind feels more and more free, more open to the possibilities of relaxation.
>
> 1
>
> You float into the clouds, completely without effort or concern. You settle into a deep and comfortable state of relaxation.
>
> And 0.

Now, we can return to Sue's sequence. She has selected the phrases "become more and more still," "sink more and more deeply into a pleasant state of relaxation," and "your mind becomes peacefully centered," and "time is like a river, each crisis passes and is forgotten." Note how these, plus such somatic phrases as "Let the tension flow . . . let tension dissolve," enhance relaxation.

SUE'S SCRIPT: Phrases Suggesting Skills, Structures, and the Deepening of Relaxation

[ISOMETRIC SQUEEZE]

Make a tight fist with your right hand.

Hold the tension . . .

Attend to the sensations of tension . . .

And let go.

Let the tension flow . . .

Imagine you are sitting on the banks of a mountain stream, your legs dangling in the water.

Let tension dissolve into the water.

Attend to the feelings of relaxation.

SINK MORE AND MORE DEEPLY INTO A PLEASANT STATE OF RELAXATION.

Tighten up the muscles in your feet and toes . . .

Let the tension build . . .

And let go.

Let the tension dissolve . . .

Let tension flow into the water.

Compare the feelings of tension and relaxation.

[BREATHING]

Take in a deep breath, filling your lungs completely.

Gently exhale.

Let the air flow out of your lips with every breath.

BECOME MORE AND MORE STILL.

The only sound you hear is the quiet flow of breath and a quiet mountain stream.

[IMAGERY]

Now, quietly attend only to the image of sitting on the banks of a cool, refreshing mountain stream.

BECOME MORE AND MORE STILL.

Your feet gently swing in the cool, refreshing water.

Tension flows down each leg, into your toes, and is dissolved and carried away by the water.

You can see the clear, sparkling water, smell its clear spray, and feel the warm sun on your skin.

YOUR MIND BECOMES PEACEFULLY CENTERED.

TIME IS LIKE A RIVER, EACH CRISIS PASSES AND IS FORGOTTEN.

Attend with all your senses to this beautiful, relaxing moment.

[MEDITATION]

Quietly attend to the coming and going of the present moment.

INTRODUCE PHRASES SUGGESTING SOMATIC SENSATIONS, SKILLS, AND STRUCTURES IN CLIENT'S SCRIPT.

Sequence Coherence

An exercise sequence that is just a random chain of calisthenics is uninteresting and easily forgotten. A number of strategies can enhance the coherence of a sequence, the degree to which separate parts fit together.

If a trainee's relaxation sequence includes more than one general approach (yoga stretching, breathing, and imagery, e.g.), elements of one approach can be *integrated* into others. For example, breathing exercises can be separately featured in a relaxation sequence or woven into isometric squeeze relaxation and yoga stretching:

Take a deep breath as you tighten up the muscles.

Hold the muscles tighter and tighter.

And as you let go, gently exhale . . .

Slowly, smoothly, and gently stretch.

Stretch farther and farther.

Gently take in a deep breath as you stretch completely.

And very slowly, smoothly, and gently release the stretch, while easily exhaling.

Similarly, if a client demonstrates proficiency at imagery, specific images symbolizing focusing, passivity, and receptivity can be integrated into other approaches, such as isometric squeeze relaxation, yoga stretching, and breathing:

> As you let go of your tension, imagine a tight ball of string slowly unwinding. Bit by bit each string relaxes as you let go of tension more and more completely. Gently and easily the entire wad becomes more and more loose.

> As you stretch, imagine you are a tree. Your arms are the branches gracefully bending in the wind. With every breeze, you bend, and release your tensions.

> You are by the seashore. As each wave approaches the shore you take a deep breath. As the wave splashes against the shore, you gently exhale and release your tensions.

An exercise can be used to *frame* a sequence. That is, an element that appears at the onset of a sequence can be repeated at the end. The end version may be modified to reflect increased focus, passivity, and receptivity. For example, a set of exercises might begin with the image of a unsettled pond, its wind-blown surface symbolizing distraction and unnecessary effortful striving. An appropriate ending could be a still, quiet pond. Similarly, one might begin and end a sequence with a deep breathing exercise. The initial exercise might be performed with some vigor and effort whereas the final version would be conducted with greater calm.

The skilled use of *metaphor* can interrelate and summarize components of an exercise and provide subtle transitions between exercises. For example, initially a yoga sequence might be described as similar to a tree bending in a wind. Later on, actual stretching instructions might be replaced with a summarizing metaphor; the relaxer stretches to the instructions "You are a tree bending in a wind . . . bending slowly, smoothly, and gently." Eventually, the same metaphor can serve as a cue for a mental imagery sequence, "Imagine in your mind a tree bending . . ." When metaphor is woven into an exercise sequence, it can serve not only as a unifying and transitional device, but as a recurring cue or reminder that the exercise sequence is becoming increasingly cognitive and passive.

Sue has introduced repeated instructions for "exhaling through lips."

SUE'S SCRIPT: Coherence

[ISOMETRIC SQUEEZE]

Make a tight fist with your right hand.

Hold the tension . . .

Attend to the sensations of tension . . .

And let go.

Let the tension flow.

Imagine you are sitting on the banks of a mountain stream, your legs dangling in the water.

Let tension dissolve into the water.

Attend to the feelings of relaxation . . .

Sink more and more deeply into a pleasant state of relaxation.

QUIETLY OPEN YOUR LIPS, AND LET TENSION FLOW WITH EVERY BREATH.

LET THE FLOW OF BREATH BE AS GENTLE AS THE FLOW OF A MOUNTAIN STREAM.

Tighten up the muscles in your feet and toes . . .

Let the tension build . . .

And let go.

Let the tension dissolve . . .

Let tension flow into the water.

Compare the feelings of tension and relaxation . . .

AGAIN, EASILY OPEN YOUR LIPS AND GENTLY LET TENSION BREATH OUT.

LET YOUR BREATH FLOW AS GENTLY AS A MOUNTAIN STREAM.

[BREATHING]

Take in a deep breath, filling your lungs completely.

Gently exhale.

Let the air flow out of your lips with every breath.

Become more and more still.

The only sound you hear is the quiet flow of breath and a quiet mountain stream.

[IMAGERY]

Now, quietly attend only to the image of sitting on the banks of a cool, refreshing mountain stream.

Become more and more still.

Your feet gently swing in the cool, refreshing water.

Tension flows down each leg, into your toes, and is dissolved and carried away by the water.

QUIETLY OPEN YOUR LIPS AND LET TENSION FLOW WITH EVERY BREATH.

THE FLOW OF BREATH IS AS GENTLE AS A MOUNTAIN STREAM.

WITH EVERY OUTGOING BREATH LET GO OF YOUR WORRIES OVER PAST AND FUTURE.

You can see the clear, sparkling water, smell its clean spray, and feel the warm sun on your your skin.

Your mind becomes peacefully centered.

Time is like a river, each crisis passes and is forgotten.

Attend with all your senses to this beautiful, relaxing moment.

[MEDITATION]

Quietly attend to the coming and going of the present moment.

AT THIS TIME ADD PHRASES TO ENHANCE SCRIPT COHERENCE.

Refinements

Anticipations of Setback

In relaxation training, setbacks are common: attention wanders, expected relaxation effects do not occur, unexpected experiences are encountered, one forgets to practice, maladaptive thoughts interfere with relaxation, coping failures in everyday life increase tension, and so on. It is useful to expect such setbacks and deal with them through special phrases introduced in your script (for example, "Distractions are normal, and can indicate that relaxation is uncovering hidden stresses; relaxation is like any other skill, it takes time to work; sometimes deeper levels of relaxation can create unexpected feelings and sensations").

In addition, one can plan ahead coping strategies for dealing with setback. One way of doing this is to introduce *cycle-enhancing imagery* at select places in your script. Such imagery (a) implicitly acknowledges that relaxation involves a cyclical process with divergent and convergent phases, and (b) affirms the redeployment of focusing, passivity, and receptivity. Examples include:

Whenever you notice you are thinking about something unrelated to relaxation, picture yourself letting go of this thought as if it were a butterfly you are holding and releasing.

Give each distracting thought to your relaxation as if you were giving it a gift.

Say to yourself, "What an interesting distraction. OK, back to my relaxation."

Say to the distraction "thank you" and return to your exercise.

Imagine dropping each distraction into a deep space as though you were dropping pebbles into a pond.

Let distracting thoughts and pictures stay in your mind if they want. But they stay in the background while you return to your exercise.

Imagine each distraction to be a form of stress release that enables you to relax better.

ADD ANTICIPATION OF SETBACK TO SCRIPT.

Relaxation Reinforcements

One way of deepening and strengthening relaxation is to introduce a few words of encouragement and support and highlight pleasurable, rewarding aspects of relaxation practice. Such reinforcements can be presented as direct statements ("Very good.") or as phrases combined with other instructions ("It is good to let go of the cares of the day."). There is a large lexicon of potentially reinforcing relaxing words, including:

Able	Competent	Good
Actualized	Complete	Great
Adjusted	Composed	Happy
Alive	Controlled	Harmonious
Answered	Coordinated	Healing
At home	Coping	Healthy
Balanced	Cozy	In control
Beautiful	Delighted	Integrated
Belonging	Effective	In touch
Blessed	Energized	Invigorated
Blissful	Enjoyable	Joyful
Calm	Even	Knowing
Capable	Exhilarated	Meaningful
Cheerful	Exultant	Natural
Collected	Fresh	Peaceful
Comfortable	Fun	Perceptive

Pleasant	Restored	Tranquil
Pleased	Rewarded	Understanding
Pleasured	Sensuous	Unified
Poised	Serene	Uplifted
Positive	Soothed	Vigorous
Recovered	Stable	Vitalized
Refreshed	Steady	Whole
Relaxed	Strengthened	Wise
Rested	Strong	Wonderful

Some reinforcing phrases include:

There is no need to push yourself, you are doing fine.

Move at a pace that feels comfortable to you.

Notice the pleasant feelings you have created.

It is OK to let yourself sink deeper into relaxation.

When you let go and attend to relaxation, you are doing well.

Take care not to introduce reinforcements for thoughts and behaviors that may not be present. For example, the reinforcement, "It is good that you are completely relaxed" may actually create needless worry and tension if one is not in fact completely relaxed. It is better to reinforce relaxation attempts ("It is good to begin to put aside the cares of the day") as well as the general direction (and not end point) of relaxation ("It is good to become more focused.").

It is important to withhold reinforcement from thoughts and behaviors not conducive to relaxation. For example, it is OK to experience distraction during a session. However, pursuing distractions for any length of time serves to reinforce the initial decision to pursue. Also, by reacting to distraction with a considerable degree of disturbance and upset, one appraises the distraction as major and important. It is better to treat distractions as passing and insignificant.

Sue's reinforcements are tied with affirmations of relaxing beliefs, values, and commitments: "In this silent moment you realize that all things come and go. It is a time of deep inner peace and joy."

ADD REINFORCING PHRASES TO SCRIPT.

Pauses and Silences

A relaxation sequence should include frequent pauses and periods of silence. It is at moments when nothing is being said or done that the effects of an exercise can begin to take hold. There are also times during an exercise when a client might want to be left in silence, for example, during a meditation. Finally, beginning relaxation trainers tend to be stingy with pauses; it is better to write in too many than too few.

Termination Segment

A sequence should not end abruptly. Gently state that the relaxation sequence is now completed. Gradually return to the outside world ("Gradually open your eyes, as if the sun were rising over the horizon") and end with a good stretch or deep breath. A termination segment can include a suggestion that the pleasant feelings of relaxation will carry over to the rest of the day.

We are now ready to take a look at Sue's script, including her anticipation of setback, reinforcing segment, pauses, and termination segment:

SUE'S COMPLETE SCRIPT Including Reinforcing Segment, Pauses, and Termination Segment

[ISOMETRIC SQUEEZE]

Make a tight fist with your right hand.

Hold the tension . . .

Attend to the sensations of tension . . .

And let go.

Let the tension flow . . .

[PAUSE]

Imagine you are sitting on the banks of a mountain stream, your legs dangling in the water.

Let tension dissolve into the water.

[PAUSE]

Attend to the feelings of relaxation . . .

[PAUSE]

Sink more and more deeply into a pleasant state of relaxation.

[PAUSE]

Quietly open your lips, and let tension flow with every breath.

[PAUSE]

Let the flow of breath be as gentle as the flow of a mountain stream.

[PAUSE]

Tighten up the muscles in your feet and toes . . .

Let the tension build . . .

And let go.

Let the tension dissolve . . .

[PAUSE]

Let tension flow into the water.

[PAUSE]

Compare the feelings of tension and relaxation . . .

[PAUSE]

Again, easily open your lips and gently let tension breathe out.

[PAUSE]

Let your breath flow as gently as a mountain stream.

[PAUSE]

[BREATHING]

Take in a deep breath, filling your lungs completely.

Gently exhale.

[PAUSE]

Let the air flow out of your lips with every breath.

[PAUSE]

Become more and more still.

[PAUSE 10 SECONDS]

The only sound you hear is the quiet flow of breath and a quiet mountain stream.

[PAUSE 10 SECONDS]

[IMAGERY]

Now, quietly attend only to the image of sitting on the banks of a cool, refreshing mountain stream.

Become more and more still.

[PAUSE]

Your feet gently swing in the cool, refreshing water.

Tension flows down each leg, into your toes, and is dissolved and carried away by the water.

[PAUSE]

Quietly open your lips and let tension flow with every breath.

The flow of breath is as gentle as a mountain stream.

[PAUSE 5 SECONDS]

With every outgoing breath let go of your worries over past and future.

[PAUSE]

You can see the clear, sparkling water, smell its clean spray, and feel the warm sun on your skin.

Your mind becomes peacefully centered.

Time is like a river, each crisis passes and is forgotten.

[PAUSE 20 SECONDS]

LET YOURSELF RELAX AT YOUR OWN PACE; IF YOUR MIND WANDERS FROM TIME TO TIME, THAT'S FINE.

[PAUSE]

Attend with all your senses to this beautiful, relaxing moment.

[PAUSE 3 MINUTES]

[MEDITATION]

Quietly attend to the coming and going of the present moment.

[PAUSE]

IF YOU ARE DISTRACTED, THAT'S OK; SIMPLY RETURN TO YOUR RELAXATION.

[PAUSE 5 SECONDS]

IN THIS SILENT MOMENT YOU REALIZE THAT ALL THINGS COME AND GO.

IT IS A TIME OF DEEP INNER PEACE AND JOY.

[PAUSE 5 MINUTES]

TAKE IN A DEEP BREATH

[PAUSE]

AND EXHALE

GENTLY LET GO OF WHAT YOU ARE ATTENDING TO

[PAUSE]

WITH EVERY OUTGOING BREATH, LET YOUR EYES SLOWLY OPEN TO THE OUTSIDE WORLD

[PAUSE]

THIS CONCLUDES THE RELAXATION SEQUENCE

ADD SCRIPT REFINEMENTS.

EVALUATING A SCRIPT

Once a script has been written, it is often useful to check for possible problems. Is it too long or too short? Are the instructions concrete and specific? Include every detail and leave very little to the imagination (except in intuitive or contemplative segments). Remember that the relaxer should not have to be concerned with filling in missing details or figuring out what ambiguous instructions mean. So instead of saying "Do some yoga stretching with your arm," say "Slowly, smoothly, and gently stretch and reach with your right arm." This instruction is far too vague: "Imagine a cool pond and relax." This one is better: "Picture yourself next to a clear, cool pond. There is barely a ripple. The water is blue. The sky is clear without a cloud. You can feel a calm wind." Examine the script for any statements you question or contradict. Avoid statements like the following:

> You will immediately recover from your cold.
>
> You will find the answer to your problem.
>
> You are now more relaxed than you have ever been before.

Frankly, a client may not immediately recover from a cold, find an answer to a problem, or become more relaxed than ever. So avoid making promises you might not be able to keep.

SAMPLE SCRIPTS

We conclude with highlights of five additional relaxation scripts. The first demonstrates that cognitive-behavioral principles can be used to enhance traditional approaches to relaxation, in this example, progressive relaxation. The second illustrates a combination of yoga, breathing, meditation, imagery, and somatic focusing exercises. The third integrates isometric squeeze, stretching, and somatic focusing in a sequence reminiscent of the ancient Chinese movement meditation, Tai Chi. It demonstrates how relaxation exercises can be designed to reflect the goals of therapy, for example, assertiveness training. The fourth script incorporates a series of exercises tailored for children. The final "creativity" script shows how relaxation can be used for purposes other than tension release.

An Enhanced Version of Progressive Relaxation

Goal: General stress management and therapy
Unifying Idea: Detecting and releasing muscle tension

> In this exercise sequence we are going to quietly look for and release sources of muscle tension. We will do this several ways, first

by actively squeezing and letting go, then letting go as we exhale and release our breath, and finally by engaging in a special type of mental imagery. Note that we shift from active to passive, not only in each exercise, but in the entire sequence.

Take in a deep breath, and tighten up your hand muscles *now*.

Hold the tension.

Notice how tension feels.

And *let go*, gently letting out all the air. That's good.

[PAUSE]

Let the tension begin to flow out of your fingers.

[PAUSE]

Study the difference between sensations of tension and relaxation.

[PAUSE]

As your fingers become more relaxed, think the words "fingers warm and heavy, fingers warm and heavy."

[PAUSE]

Attend to the sensations of relaxation as you sink into relaxation.

[REPEAT TWICE FOR EVERY MAJOR MUSCLE GROUP]

And now we move to exercises that are more gentle.

Slowly take in a deep breath.

[PAUSE]

Notice any feelings of tension you may have.

[PAUSE]

And gently *let go*.

[PAUSE]

Let tightness flow out as you exhale.

[PAUSE]

Let the flow of air bring warmth and heaviness to your fingers, hands, arms, and feet as you sink deeper into relaxation.

[PAUSE]

Compare the subtle sensations of tension and relaxation.

[PAUSE]

It's OK to let yourself have feelings of warmth, tingling, or heaviness.

[CONTINUE WITH REPETITIONS AND SLIGHT VARIATIONS]

As we continue, our exercises become more and more passive and quiet.

Let your breathing continue easily and unforced.

[PAUSE]

Quietly attend to your hands and fingers.
[PAUSE]
Imagine warm stream of air gently caressing your hands and fingers.
[PAUSE]
The flow of air dissolves your tensions and carries them away.
[PAUSE]
Very slowly and gently, the flow of air starts at your wrist and smoothes out remaining tension all the way to the finger tips. Picture tension as tiny wrinkles that are easily smoothed into relaxation.
[PAUSE 15 SECONDS]
See if you tell the difference between very slight feelings of tension and relaxation.
[PAUSE 15 SECONDS]
Let yourself sink more and more deeply into a pleasant state of relaxation. Your mind focuses more and more on the calm you have created.
[REPEAT FOR ARMS, BACK, SHOULDERS, NECK, FACE, LEGS, AND FEET]

A Yoga Stretching Meditation

Goal: Recovering from a hectic day
Unifying Idea: A palm tree bowing in the wind

Imagine you are a palm tree standing by the ocean beach. As the wind blows, big waves crash against the shore. Each wave releases its tension as the water runs up and dissolves into the sand. The warm sun shines overhead, a source of life and energy for all the world.
[PAUSE]
A long, slow gust of wind sighs through the leaves.
[PAUSE]
Slowly, smoothly, and gently bow over and stretch completely.
[PAUSE 10 SECONDS]
Feel the stretch completely, all along your arms and torso.
[COMPLETE STRETCH]
As the gust subsides, gently unstretch and release your tension.
[PAUSE]
You end your stretch and a wave crashes against the shore, releasing its energy into the sand.

[PAUSE]

The sun overhead bathes you in an ocean of peaceful clear light.

[PAUSE]

The wind begins to grow more gentle.

[PAUSE]

Even more easily than before, slowly reach up and stretch. Stretch all the way, barely moving a leaf.

[PAUSE]

Gently return to your upright position, as a wave quietly releases its tension against the shore.

At the end of the stretch, let yourself settle into stillness in the warm sun.

[COMPLETE STRETCH. REPEAT FOR NECK, FACE, AND LEGS]

Let yourself enjoy this relaxation. You have the capacity within for creating peace and calm. Let your mind attend to the good sensations you have created.

[PAUSE]

The waves have settled into quiet ripples lapping against the shore.

[PAUSE]

As you let yourself sink deeper into a pleasant state of inner calm, very slowly and easily rock back and forth to the easy rhythm of the waves.

[PAUSE 10 SECONDS]

Let your movements be so gentle that they barely stir the air.

[PAUSE 10 SECONDS]

You have few cares or concerns as you attend only to this rocking motion.

[PAUSE]

Quietly overhead, the sun continues to touch all with its delicate and gentle rays.

[PAUSE]

The wind becomes completely quiet and the ocean is still.

[PAUSE]

Let your body become completely motionless as you settle into a deeper calm.

[PAUSE]

It is good to let your mind center on the warm sun against your skin. It reminds you that you can trust your innermost thoughts and feelings.

[PAUSE]

Whenever your mind wanders, that's OK.

[PAUSE]

Gently return to the sun as it bathes you in peaceful life-giving light.

[PAUSE]

This is your meditation focus for the next five minutes.

[PAUSE 5 MINUTES]

A Movement Exercise

Goal: Preparing for an assertive encounter
Unifying Idea: Flowing with the moment

Attend to the muscles in your right hand and fingers.

Make a tight fist *now*.

[PAUSE]

Attend to the feelings of tightness.

[PAUSE]

By holding and keeping your thoughts and feelings to yourself, you create needless tension.

[PAUSE]

And *let go*.

Feel the flow of energy as you release the resistance you have created.

[PAUSE]

There is nothing for you to do but attend to the good feelings of relaxation.

[PAUSE]

Notice the difference between tension and relaxation.

[PAUSE 30 SECONDS]

And now, slowly, smoothly, and gently open the fingers of your right hand.

[PAUSE]

Let them stretch more and more completely.

[PAUSE]

Imagine energy flowing down your hands, into your fingers, and out of your fingertips.

[PAUSE]

As your fingers open, you open to the world.

[PAUSE]

As energy is released, slowly, smoothly, and gently release your stretch.

[PAUSE]

Very gently return your fingers to their original resting position.

[PAUSE]

Take your time, let yourself flow easily and gracefully.

[REPEAT ISOMETRIC SQUEEZE AND STRETCHES FOR ARMS, BACK, NECK, SHOULDERS, AND FACE]

Good. Continue attending to your right hand. While remaining still, let warm and tingling sensations spread from your hands to your fingers.

[PAUSE]

Let these feelings slowly dissolve feelings of tension and carry them away through your fingertips.

[PAUSE]

Notice the good feelings you create by not blocking the flow of the moment.

[PAUSE]

It's OK to be open to your feelings. They are good and can be trusted. You do not have to hold them to yourself.

[PAUSE]

For the next three minutes quietly attend to the warmth and tingling in your hands and fingers.

[PAUSE 3 MINUTES]

A Children's Relaxation

Goal: To relax in the middle of the day
Unifying Idea: The train

Imagine you are an old steam engine train taking a long trip into the countryside. All the passengers have been seated. You are about ready to leave the station. Friendly crowds wave to you and you smile and wave back. The moment is alive with energy and excitement.

As steam begins to build in your giant engine, take in a deep breath and tighten up your shoulders. Let the tension build. Hold the tension. And relax and exhale. As you release a puff of steam, imagine giving all your cars a gentle tug. The train begins to move and coast along the tracks. You can begin to relax and let your muscles become more and more limp. There is nothing you have to do but coast along the tracks.

Now, it is time to move a little bit faster. Take in a breath and tighten up your shoulders. Let the tension build. And let go, tugging your cars again. The train coasts along and you relax. Notice the good feelings as you become more calm.

[ISOMETRIC SQUEEZE RELAXATION EXERCISES ARE REPEATED FOR THE BACK, NECK, FACE, ARMS, AND LEGS]

You are now rolling through the countryside. You can relax even more because the train is moving on its own. The engine chugs smoothly and evenly and little clouds of steam float into the sky.

Let your breathing become smooth and easy. Quietly open your lips, and slowly exhale. See if you can make the flow of steam so smooth that it barely stirs the air. With every outgoing breath, let yourself relax. As you move along the track, you move further from the worries of the day, deeper into the peaceful countryside. There is nothing you have to do but breathe slowly and evenly.

[PAUSE]

You have traveled deep into the country. All the things that cause trouble for you are far in the distance. The track has become more smooth and you can barely hear or feel the chugging of the engine. Your breathing is very calm and even. Restful hills roll past, covered with soft green grass, trees, and an occasional pond. Contented sheep graze lazily. You can feel the warm friendly sun against your skin. It feels good and comfortable. Look at the world silently flowing past. Notice all the wonderful relaxing things you can see and hear.

[CONTINUE WITH IMAGERY FOR 3 MINUTES.]

The sun is beginning to set. As evening comes, the colors outside become gray. A soft blanket of silence covers everything. All you feel is the peaceful rocking of the train and your breath slowly flowing in and out. Let yourself easily rock, like a train rocking on the tracks. Let each rocking motion be so quiet that it can barely be noticed. For the next few remaining minutes, quietly attend to your rocking motion, slowly back and forth. Whenever your mind wanders, that's OK. Gently rock back and forth. That is all you need to attend to. It can be good to take rest from the problems of the day. A rest can give you more power to do the things you want. Let yourself relax and rock for the next few minutes.

[PAUSE 2 MINUTES]

A Creativity Exercise

Goal: Facilitate "idea generation"
Unifying Idea: The black stone

Take in a full, deep breath and quietly exhale.

It is time to put aside effort and deliberate thought.

You are about to embark upon a journey into your mind.

Once again, take in a complete breath, and exhale, this time a bit more gently.

[PAUSE 10 SECONDS]

You will have an opportunity to ask a question important to you and silently let answers come from an inner source of creativity.

[PAUSE]

Continue to breathe fully and easily. Let each breath become increasingly calm.

[PAUSE 10 SECONDS]

Take your time. There is no need to hurry. Let yourself become centered for your inner journey.

[PAUSE 1 MINUTE]

Imagine you are at the edge of a forest. The air is calm with anticipation and the sun waits silently overhead. Occasionally the song of a bird echoes into silence.

[PAUSE 10 SECONDS]

In front of you is the opening of a cave. You slowly approach and gaze inside. A long flight of granite stairs descends into darkness.

[PAUSE]

Here is where your journey begins. Even though the cave is dark, you feel reassured. Calmly and confidently, you begin your descent. One step at a time.

[PAUSE]

A quiet voice starts counting down, from 5 to 1. With each number, you gently breathe in and out, and descend a step. With each number you let yourself become more centered, more open to the possibilities ahead.

[PAUSE]

5

You breathe, and take one step.

[PAUSE]

4

It is safe to let yourself be completely free from the constraints of the outside world.

[PAUSE]

3

Your mind becomes increasingly clear.

[PAUSE]

2

The cares of the outside world seem so distant.

[PAUSE]

1

At the end of the stairs you encounter a mysterious dark shining stone, as clear as a mirror, reaching from floor to roof.

[PAUSE]

Let your attention become centered into the darkness ahead. It almost seems as if you were looking into the infinite expanse of space. The stone seems deep with mystery. It seems alive.

[PAUSE]

Quietly attend to the stone and gently ask your question.

And simply wait.

[PAUSE]

Say nothing. Do nothing. Expect nothing.

[PAUSE]

A creative source deep within holds the potential for answering your questions.

[PAUSE]

Attend to what the stone has to reveal to you, in whatever way or form it desires.

[PAUSE 10 SECONDS]

And whenever the stone responds, you acknowledge by nodding silently.

[PAUSE]

Continue attending, without thinking or analyzing any response.

[PAUSE 10 SECONDS]

Whenever your mind wanders, that's OK. Gently return.

[PAUSE]

This is your focus for the next 10 minutes.

[PAUSE 10 MINUTES]

APPENDIX C

Abbreviated Client Relaxation Manual

The following relaxation instructions present the core ideas of the Relaxation Protocol in terms readily understood by clients. A therapist must first teach an adequate series of relaxation exercises and help the client select those that are preferred. Once a selection has been made, the client can develop a personalized relaxation program using the following instructions with minimal therapist assistance.

HOW TO ENHANCE YOUR RELAXATION SEQUENCE WITH SETUPS AND LINKUPS

One way of making your relaxation program work better is to introduce special *relaxation setups and linkups*. A setup contains a series of exercises and phrases that come before the exercises you have chosen to practice. Such an introduction sets the stage for relaxation and helps establish a frame of mind conducive to more rewarding relaxation experiences. For example, if you have decided to practice five isometric squeeze exercises, you might begin with a series of setup exercises that focus on the relaxing fantasy of a faraway and restful island. A relaxation linkup is based on and similar to a setup. However, it comes in the middle of a relaxation sequence, between sets of exercises. Linkups also help maintain an appropriate relaxation setting and mood.

    Setups and linkups serve an important function in relaxation. They help pull exercises together into a unified whole. They help tie exercises to whatever attitudes and personal philosophies you may have that are conducive to relaxation. Finally, setups and linkups help make a series of exercises more enjoyable to practice.

The rules for making setups and linkups are simple. You just write a script that lists the words, ideas, and exercises you want to include. Before we present the instructions on how to do this, let's examine some sample relaxation programs.

Example 1

Setup

Close your eyes and imagine you are on a peaceful island.

The breeze is remarkably peaceful and relaxing.

You can feel the cool air on your skin as the wind gently blows and subsides.

You become more and more centered in this peaceful setting, enjoying the peaceful and refreshing wind.

In the following exercises, let your breath become as smooth and gentle as the wind.

Exercise Sequence

Bowing and breathing

Breathing in through nose

Breathing out through lips

Linkup

Imagine you are still on your distant peaceful island.

The wind has settled.

Everything is completely quiet.

You can see the moon overhead like a brilliant silver coin.

Everything is so still.

All your cares and concerns seem so distant and far away.

This moment is deeply peaceful and reassuring.

Exercise Sequence

Focused breathing

Meditation (on a mental image of the reflected moon)

In this example, notice how the setups and linkups establish the mood and setting for the breathing and meditation exercises. They contain special words, like "peaceful" and "reassuring," that enhance relaxation. In practicing this sequence, you could read the setup and linkup instructions before practicing and continuing. Or, you could simply close your eyes and let your imagination be guided by the instructions.

In the following example, the setup and linkup actually contains a small relaxation exercise.

Example 2

Setup

Begin by taking in a deep breath and making a tight fist with your right fist.

Exhale through your lips and let go.

Imagine tension dissolving and flowing out with every outgoing breath.

Let yourself sink more and more deeply into a peaceful state.

Exercise Sequence

Hand squeeze

Arm squeeze

Back squeeze

Linkup

Let yourself settle more and more deeply with every outgoing breath.

Gently open your lips, and again let tension dissolve and flow out with every outgoing breath.

Remember that you have the capacity within to let go of tension and enjoy the rewards of deep relaxation.

Exercise Sequence

Back of neck squeeze

Shoulder squeeze

Face squeeze

Front of neck squeeze

Notice how a simple breathing exercise introduces and ties together a sequence of isometric squeeze exercises. This program also illustrates another way of using setups and linkups. One powerful way of making relaxation more effective is to introduce from time to time a *personal philosophy* that is conducive to relaxation. The philosophy introduced here is, "Remember that you have the capacity within to let go of tension and enjoy the rewards of deep relaxation."

We are now ready to learn how to construct an effective relaxation program. First, select the sequence of exercises you want to practice. Then, develop your setups and linkups using the following steps.

1. Select your unifying idea
2. Select and order exercises for your Setup and Linkup
3. Introduce your unifying idea
4. Introduce deepening suggestions

Step 1: Select Your Unifying Idea

An exercise sequence acquires structure and meaning from a unifying idea, a statement of a sequence's overall justification, what it is all about. There are five possible types of unifying ideas which we will explain on the following pages.

1. Exercise Rationale (explanation why it works)
2. Exercise Goal
3. Affirmation of a Personal Relaxation Philosophy
4. Relaxation Symbolic Image
5. Relaxation Story

Often, a unifying idea is little more than the rationale or explanation of how a procedure works. For example, a practitioner of isometric squeeze relaxation would probably think of each exercise enhancing ability to discriminate and let go of tension. Additional examples include: "Relaxation loosens muscle tension," "The flow of blood to my muscles increases," and "Relaxation enables me to divert attention from the day's concern to the present moment."

A relaxation goal can be simply the pragmatic reason for practicing relaxation, for example: "stress release," "combating insomnia," "waking up refreshed for the day," "preparing for work," or even "prayer" or "communing with nature." A goal can also be artistic expression. Here, constructing or practicing an exercise becomes a special and somewhat unusual art form, one with the dual goals of creating a thing of beauty and evoking relaxation. Put differently, techniques of relaxation become an expressive medium, analogous to the words of a poet, the paints of an artist, or the dance steps of a choreographer.

Unifying ideas can be affirmations of personal relaxation philosophies," for example, "Live in the present moment," "God's will be done," "Let go of that which cannot be changed," or "Trust the powers within you."

They can symbolize what relaxation means to you. The theme of a *peaceful woods* might stand for many aspects of a relaxation sequence. For example, a gentle breeze might symbolize breathing exercises; trees slowly bowing in the wind, stretching exercises; the sun warming the leaves, physical sensations of "warmth and heaviness"; and the silence of approaching evening, a meditative focus of attention. Note how these images are not only peaceful in their own right, but suggestive of specific relaxation exercises. In another example, the theme of *waves crashing on the shore* can symbolize a variety of exercises. The energy that builds and releases with each crashing wave can suggest the tension-release cycle of isometric squeeze relaxation (or inhalation and exhalation of deep breathing). The dissolving of each wave into the sand can be linked with physical relaxation suggestions of "heaviness, tingling, and dissolving tension." And the quiet wind that flows across the water before the next wave can suggest focused breathing.

A unifying idea can be something of a very simple story or changing image, providing all elements are linked to relaxation exercises, change in a direction of increased relaxation, and end in deeper relaxation. For example, the theme of waves crashing on the shore just mentioned is a bit of a story—a wave builds up, crashes, dissolves into the sand, and a quiet wind blows. Other examples include: "a leaf floating down the river," "a bubble rising to the surface of the pond," or "the sun dissolving a block of ice into a puddle of water."

Before concluding this discussion, it is useful to note that unifying ideas can be put in your own words, or embodied in a passage from a song, poem, prayer, or piece of literature you have found to be particularly peaceful. You can use the entire passage as an introduction to your relaxation sequence or introduce parts of it into each exercise.

WHAT IS YOUR UNIFYING IDEA?

Step 2: Select and Order Exercises

Next, you need to select which exercises you want to include in your setups and linkups. As few or as many can be chosen, although it is a good idea to pick exercises that seem to "flow into" your relaxation program of exercises and are compatible with your unifying idea.

Step 3: Introduce Your Unifying Idea

You are now ready to introduce phrases that express your unifying idea. Try to weave your unifying idea into the exercises selected. To illustrate this, we have taken each of the five types of unifying ideas discussed earlier and presented them as a setup for the same isometric squeeze exercises:

Example 1

Setup

[Unifying Idea: Relaxation rationale of diverting attention from the day's concerns]

In this series of exercises, you will attend to a variety of pleasing and satisfying muscle sensations associated with relaxation.

These are sensations you create simply by tensing and letting go.

Let yourself attend to and study these sensations.

See if you can tell when a muscle is relaxed and when it is tense.

As you become more focused on your task, you become less aware of your daily concerns.

Exercise Sequence

Hand squeeze
Arm squeeze
Back squeeze
Shoulder squeeze

Example 2

Setup

[Unifying Idea: Relaxation goal of preparing for sleep]

In this series of exercises you will learn to let go of tension and sink into a deeper and deeper state of drowsiness and relaxation.

Each time you tense up and let go, you release some of the tension that keeps you from sinking deeper into a pleasant drowsy state.

Exercise Sequence

Hand squeeze
Arm squeeze
Back squeeze
Shoulder squeeze

Example 3

Setup

[Unifying Idea: A personal relaxation philosophy]

In this series of exercises you will create and let go of muscle tension.

Throughout the day you create unnecessary tension by needlessly trying to control matters which are perhaps beyond your control.

In this exercise we begin by tensing up, and then letting go of the needless control and tension you have created.

Notice that in these exercises, as in life, you are still in control even when you let go of tension.

Exercise Sequence

Hand squeeze
Arm squeeze
Back squeeze
Shoulder squeeze

Example 4

Setup

[Unifying Idea: The symbolic idea of an unwinding ball of string]

Imagine tension as a tightly coiled ball of string.

As you let go of tension, the ball slowly uncoils, bit by bit.

Exercise Sequence

Hand squeeze
Arm squeeze
Back squeeze
Shoulder squeeze

Example 5

Setup

> [Unifying Idea: A bubble rising in a pond]
>
> Begin by tightening up your muscles.
>
> Then let go.
>
> As you relax, imagine a bubble being released from the floor of a pond.
>
> It slowly rises as you become more relaxed.
>
> Each time you tense, imagine the bubble becoming lighter and lighter, rising closer to the surface.
>
> And when you are finished, simply attend to the bubble, gently floating on the surface.

Exercise Sequence

> Hand squeeze
> Arm squeeze
> Back squeeze
> Shoulder squeeze

The following examples include setups that are a bit more elaborate. Notice how setups can include components of the exercises that follow.

Example 1

Setup

> [Unifying Idea: The candle]
>
> Picture tension as a hard ball of candle wax.
>
> Frozen within are the cares and hassles of the day.
>
> Now, take a deep breath and make a fist with your right hand.
>
> Let your muscles become as tight as hard wax.
>
> Notice the sensations of tension.
>
> And let go and exhale.
>
> Imagine the candle is lit.
>
> Let the tension flow as the wax by the flame begins to melt.
>
> Notice the sensations of relaxation you have created.
>
> Let your fingers and hand become soft and warm, soft and heavy as wax begins to flow and release its tensions.

Exercise Sequence

Hand squeeze
Arm squeeze
Back squeeze
Shoulder squeeze
Back of neck squeeze
Face squeeze
Front of neck squeeze

Linkup

Let each breath become slow, smooth, and full.

As you become more calm and centered.

Imagine the delicate dance of the candle flame.

Let each outgoing breath begin to dissolve the tensions of the day.

And let the stream of breath gently flow past the candle flame barely enough to make it flicker.

Exercise Sequence

Bowing and breathing
Arm swing breathing
Deep breathing

Example 2

Setup

[Unifying Idea: The palm tree in the wind]

Imagine you are a palm tree bowing gently in the wind.

You are on a very peaceful island, far away from any cares and concerns.

The wind blows, and subsides.

As the wind begins to blow, gently stretch.

Stretch farther and farther, feeling a good complete stretch.

And as the wind subsides, gently unstretch, releasing your tension.

Exercise Sequence

Arm and side stretch
Back stretch
Shoulder stretch
Back of neck stretch
Face stretch

NOW, INCLUDE YOUR UNIFYING IDEA IN YOUR SETUP AND LINKUP.

Step 4: Introduce Deepening Suggestions

Setups and linkups can be enhanced by adding phrases that suggest: (1) relaxing physical sensations, (2) relaxation skills of focusing, passivity, and receptivity, (3) personal relaxation philosophies, and (4) rewarding feelings that go with relaxation. You might want to include words loosely suggestive of a variety of physical relaxation sensations that can accompany relaxation:

Bathed	High	Sinking
Caressed	Light	Slack
Cool	Limber	Sleepy
Dissolving	Limp	Slow
Drowsy	Liquid	Smooth
Elastic	Loose	Soft
Flexible	Massaged	Supple
Floating	Mellow	Throbbing
Flowing	Melting	Tingling
Heavy	Sedate	Warm

The following words are loosely suggestive of focusing, passivity, and receptivity (note that some of these words also suggest physical relaxation suggestions):

FOCUSING

Absorbed	Conscious	Mindful
Alert	Contemplative	One-pointed
At one	Deep	Pure
Attentive	Distant	Quiet
Awake	Engrossed	Radiant
Aware	Entranced	Silent
Bright	Far Away	Single-minded
Captivated	Fascinated	Still
Centered	Focused	Stimulated
Charmed	Glowing	Transparent
Cleansed	Interested	Undistracted
Clear	Lucid	
Concentrated	Meditative	

PASSIVITY

At ease	Leisurely	Selfless
Carefree	Letting be	Settled
Contented	Letting go	Simple
Detached	Listless	Spontaneous
Easy	Motionless	Surrendering
Escaped	Passive	Unbothered
Forgetting	Patient	Unencumbered
Free	Pausing	Unforced
Gentle	Playful	Unhurried
Gratified	Released	Untroubled
Indifferent	Relieved	Unworried
Laid back	Satisfied	

RECEPTIVITY

Accepting	Immortal	Rejuvenated
Amazed	Infinite	Renewed
Assured	Innocent	Reverent
Awe	Insightful	Safe
Boundless	Inspired	Secure
Childlike	Intuitive	Speechless
Confident	Liberated	Spiritual
Cosmic	Loving	Thankful
Creative	Mysterious	Timeless
Dreamy	Mystical	Touched
Ecstatic	New	Transcendent
Elated	Open	Transformed
Encouraged	Optimistic	Trusting
Enraptured	Prayerful	Unafraid
Eternal	Profound	Wonder
Expansive	Reassured	Wordless
Glorious	Reborn	Worshipful
Hopeful	Receptive	

You can enhance your setups and linkups by introducing phrases that incorporate such deepening words. Some examples might include:

Let your fingers become more and more warm *(physical sensation)*

Let your body feel lighter and lighter *(physical sensation)*

You are becoming more centered. *(focusing)*

Your mind is more attentive. *(focusing)*

Practice easily and effortlessly. *(passivity)*

Experience "letting be." *(passivity)*

You feel increasingly open to possibilities. *(receptivity)*

Trust the hidden processes of relaxation. *(receptivity)*

Setups and linkups can be particularly effective when they affirm relaxing beliefs, values, or commitments you may have. Some examples of phrases noting personal relaxation philosophies include:

My selfish worries are distractions that fog awareness of a deeper reality.

God loves me and has a plan for my life.

The meaning of life becomes more apparent to me in the quiet of relaxation.

My urgent concerns seem less important when seen in broader perspective.

There are more important things than my everyday hassles.

At the deepest level I can feel at peace with myself—I am an OK person.

I choose to live one day at a time and not worry about things that cannot be changed.

I chose to quit creating unnecessary pain and tension for myself by ignoring my true feelings.

God's will be done.

If a poem or passage of literature expresses what relaxation means to you, you might incorporate portions of it in your script.

Finally, try to introduce a few phrases that highlight additional pleasurable and rewarding experiences you might have while relaxing. Some rewarding words include:

Able	Capable	Effective
Actualized	Cheerful	Energized
Adjusted	Collected	Enjoyable
Alive	Comfortable	Even
Answered	Competent	Exhilarated
At home	Complete	Exultant
Balanced	Composed	Fresh
Beautiful	Controlled	Fun
Belonging	Coordinated	Good
Blessed	Coping	Great
Blissful	Cozy	Happy
Calm	Delighted	Harmonious

Healing	Pleased	Stable
Healthy	Pleasured	Steady
In control	Poised	Strengthened
Integrated	Positive	Strong
In touch	Recovered	Tranquil
Invigorated	Refreshed	Understanding
Joyful	Relaxed	Unified
Knowing	Rested	Uplifted
Meaningful	Restored	Vigorous
Natural	Rewarded	Vitalized
Peaceful	Sensuous	Whole
Perceptive	Serene	Wise
Pleasant	Soothed	Wonderful

NOW INTRODUCE PHRASES SUGGESTING RELAXING PHYSICAL SENSATIONS, SKILLS, PERSONAL PHILOSOPHIES, AND REWARDING EXPERIENCES IN YOUR SETUPS AND LINKUPS. IF YOU WISH, USE WORDS AND PHRASES FROM YOUR WORKSHEETS.

We conclude with a somewhat more complicated exercise sequence based on the unifying idea of a mountain stream. This sequence demonstrates a series of linkups all related to a single setup. Notice how the exercises become more focused, passive, and open or receptive. The sequence begins with isometric squeeze relaxation and continues through breathing, imagery, and meditation. Each linkup also changes in this direction, deepening the effect of the exercises. See if you can tell how the rules we have described were applied.

Setup

Make a tight fist with your right hand.

Hold the tension . . .

Attend to the sensations of tension . . .

And let go.

Let the tension flow . . .

[PAUSE]

Imagine you are sitting on the banks of a mountain stream, your legs dangling in the water.

Let tension dissolve into the water.

[PAUSE]

Attend to the feelings of relaxation . . .

[PAUSE]

Sink more and more deeply into a pleasant state of relaxation.

[PAUSE]

Quietly open your lips, and let tension flow with every breath.

[PAUSE]

Let the flow of breath be as gentle as the low of mountain stream.

[PAUSE]

Tighten up the muscles in your feet and toes . . .

Let the tension build . . .

And let go.

Let the tension dissolve . . .

[PAUSE]

Let tension flow into the water.

[PAUSE]

Compare the feelings of tension and relaxation . . .

Exercise Sequence

Arm squeeze
Back squeeze
Shoulder squeeze
Back of neck squeeze
Face squeeze
Front of neck squeeze
Chest and stomach squeeze
Leg squeeze

Linkup

Again, easily open your lips and gently let tension breathe out.

[PAUSE]

Let your breath flow as gently as a mountain stream.

[PAUSE]

Take in a deep breath, filling your lungs completely.

Gently exhale.

[PAUSE]

Let the air flow out of your lips with every breath.

[PAUSE]

Become more and more still.

[PAUSE 10 SECONDS]

The only sound you hear is the quiet flow of breath and a quiet mountain stream.

Exercise Sequence

Breathing in through nose

Breathing out through lips

Deep breathing

Focused breathing

Linkup

Now, quietly attend only to the image of sitting on the banks of a cool, refreshing mountain stream.

Become more and more still.

[PAUSE]

Your feet gently swing in the cool, refreshing water.

Tension flows down each leg, into your toes, and is dissolved and carried away by the water.

Time is like a river, each crisis passes and is forgotten.

[PAUSE]

Quietly open your lips and let tension flow with every breath.

The flow of breath is as gentle as a mountain stream.

[PAUSE 5 SECONDS]

With every outgoing breath let go of your worries over past and future.

[PAUSE]

You can see the clear, sparkling water, smell its clean spray, and feel the warm sun on your skin.

Your mind becomes peacefully centered.

[PAUSE 20 SECONDS]

Let yourself relax at your own pace;

If your mind wanders from time to time, that's fine.

[PAUSE]

Exercise Sequence

Continue with mental imagery of a refreshing mountain stream.

Include all your senses.

Imagine the clear, blue sky, the green grass, the sound of the wind and birds, etc.

Linkup

Quietly let go of what you are attending to.

The waters of the stream grow more still.

The air is completely quiet.

Let your breathing become more and more calm, your mind more and more centered.

With every breath you move farther from the cares of the past and future.

Your mind becomes absorbed in the present.

The air is clear.

Your mind feels fresh.

Your attention centers on a tiny swirl of water in the center of the stream.

Exercise Sequence

Meditate on the unchanging swirl of water in front of you.

Whenever you are distracted, simply and calmly return your attention.

Again and again.

That is all you have to do.

Attend to the tiny swirl of water.

HOW TO EVALUATE YOUR SETUPS AND LINKUPS

Once your setups and linkups and been completed, it is often useful to check for possible problems. First, make sure they are related. A good linkup should follow from the preceding setup. If you have several linkups, each should flow from the preceding, and each should suggest deeper relaxation. In addition, are the instructions concrete and specific? Include every detail and leave very little to the imagination. Remember that you should not have to be concerned with filling in missing details or figuring out what ambiguous instructions mean. So instead of saying "Do some yoga stretching with your arm," say "Slowly, smoothly, and gently stretch and reach with your right arm." This instruction is far too vague: "Imagine a cool pond and relax." This one is better: "Picture yourself next to a clear, cool pond. There is barely a ripple. The water is blue. The sky is clear without a cloud. You can feel a calm wind."

Examine the script for any statements you question or contradict. Avoid statements like the following:

> You will immediately recover from your cold.
> You will find the answer to your problem.
> You are now more relaxed than you have ever been before.

Frankly, you may not immediately recover from a cold, find an answer to a problem, or become more relaxed than ever before. So, avoid making promises you might not be able to keep.

References

Appley, M. H., & Trumbull, R. (1967). *Psychological stress: Issues in research*. New York: Appleton-Century-Crofts.

Bandura, A. (1969). *Principles of behavior modification*. New York: Holt, Rinehart and Winston.

Barber, T. X. (1984). Hypnosis, deep relaxation, and active relaxation: Data, theory, and clinical applications. In R. L. Woolfolk & P. M. Lehrer (Eds.), *Principles and practice of stress management*. pp. 142–187. New York: Guilford.

Barber, T. X. & Wilson, S. C. (1978/1979). The Barber Suggestibility Scale and the Creative Imagination Scale. *American Journal of Clinical Hypnosis, 21,* 84–108.

Beck, A. T. (1976). *Cognitive therapy and the emotional disorders.* New York: New American Library. Benson, H, Beary, J. F., & Carol, M. P. The relaxation response. *Psychiatry,* 1974, *37,* 37–46.

Bedrosian, R. C., & Beck, A. T. (1980). Principles of cognitive therapy. In M. J. Mahoney (Ed.), *Psychotherapy process: Current issues and future, directions* pp. 127–152. New York: Plenum

Benson, H. (1975). *The relaxation response.* New York: Morrow.

Benson, H., & Friedman, R. (1985). A rebuttal to the conclusions of David S. Holmes's article: Meditation and somatic arousal reduction. *American Psychologist, 40,* 725–728.

Bernstein, D., & Borkovec, T. (1973). *Progressive relaxation training: A manual for the helping professions.* Champaign, IL: Research Press.

Bloomfield, H. H., Cain, M. P., & Jaffe, D. T. (1975). *TM: Discovering inner energy and overcoming stress.* New York: Delacorte.

Borkovec, T. D. (1987). *The Cognitive-Somatic Inventory.* Unpublished manuscript. Pennsylvania State University, University Park, PA.

Borkovec, T. D., & Bernstein, D. (1989). Foreword, in J. C. Smith, *Relaxation Dynamics: A cognitive-behavioral approach to relaxation.* Champaign, IL: Research Press.

Borkovec, T. D., Johnson, M. C., & Block, D. L. (1984). Evaluating experimental designs in relaxation research. In R. Woolfolk & P. M. Lehrer, *Principles and practice of stress management,* pp. 368–403. New York: Guilford.

Borkovec, T., & Sides, J. K. (1979). Critical procedural variables related to the physiological effects of progressive relaxation: A review. *Behaviour Research and Therapy, 17,* 119–125.

Brown, D. P., Forte, M., Rich, P., & Epstein, G. (1982). Phenomenological differences among self-hypnosis, mindfulness meditation, and imaging. *Imagination, Cognition, and Personality, 2,* 291–309.

Budzynski, T. H. (1974). *Relaxation training program.* New York: BMA Audio Cassettes.

Cannon, W. B. (1932). *The wisdom of the body.* New York: Norton (2nd ed.).

Carrington, P. (1978). *Clinical standardized meditation instructor's manual and self-regulating course.* Kendall Park, NJ: Pace Systems.

Carrington, P., Collings, G., Benson, H., Robinson, H., Wood, L., Lehrer, P. Woolfolk, R., & Cole, W. (1980). The use of meditation-relaxation techniques for the management of stress in a working population. *Journal of Occupational Medicine, 22,* 221–231.

Cattell, R. B. (1957). *Personality and motivation: Structure and measurement.* New York: World Book Co.

Cattell, R. B., Eber, H. W., and Tatsouka, M. M. (1970). *Handbook for the sixteen personality factor questionnaire.* Institute for Personality and Ability Testing, Champaign, IL.

Charlesworth, E. A., & Nathan, R. G. (1982). *Stress management.* Houston: Biobehavioral Publications.

Conze, E. (1959). *Buddhism: Its essence and development.* New York: Harper & Row.

Corby, J. C., Roth, W. T., Zarcone, V. P., & Kopell, B. S. (1978). Psychophysiological correlates of the practice of Tantric yoga meditation. *Archives of General Psychiatry, 35,* 571–577.

Crits-Christoph, P., & Singer, J. L. (1981). Imagery in cognitive-behavior therapy: Research and application. *Clinical Psychology Review, 1,* 19–32.

Curtis, J. W. (1984). Motivation to continue meditation and the ability to sustain nonanalytic attention. Unpublished Master's thesis, Roosevelt University.

Davidson, R. & Goleman, D. (1977). The role of attention in meditation and hypnosis: A psychobiological perspective on transformation of consciousness. *International Journal of Clinical and Experimental Hypnosis, 25,* 291–308.

Davidson, R. J., & Schwartz, G. E. (1976). Psychobiology of relaxation and related states: A multiprocess theory. In D. I. Mostofsky (Ed.) *Behavior control and the modification of physiological activity.* Englewood Cliffs, NJ: Prentice-Hall.

Delongis, A., Coyne, J. C., Dakof, G., Folkman, S., & Lazarus, R. S. (1982). Relationship of daily hassles, uplifts, and major life events to health status. *Health Psychology, 1,* 119–136.

Edmonston, W. E. (1981). *Hypnosis and relaxation* New York: Wiley.

Edmonston, W. E. (1986). *The induction of hypnosis.* New York: Wiley.

Eliade, M. (1969). *Patanjali and yoga.* New York: Funk & Wagnalls.

Ellis, A. (1984). The place of meditation in cognitive-behavior therapy and rational-emotive therapy. In D. Shapiro and R. Walsh (Eds.); pp. 761–763. *Meditation: Classic and contemporary perspectives.* New York: Aldine.

Ellis, A. (1962). *Reason and emotion in psychotherapy.* New York: Lyle Stuart.
Ellis, A., & Grieger, R. (1977) *Handbook of rational-emotive therapy.* New York: Springer.
Erickson, M. H., Rossi, E. L., & Rossi, S. I. (1976). *Hypnotic realities.* New York: Irvington.
Fitzgerald, E. T. (1966). The measurement of openness to experience: A study of regression in the service of the ego. *Journal of Personality and Social Psychology, 4,* 655–663.
Freud, S. (1913). "On beginning the treatment." In Strachey, J. (Ed.) *The Standard Edition of the Complete Psychological Works of Sigmund Freud,* Vol. XII. London: Hogarth. (1958).
Freud, S. (1920). "A note on the prehistory of the technique of analysis." In Strachey, J. (Ed) (1955) *The Standard Edition of the Complete Psychological Works of Sigmund Freud,* Vol XVIII. London: Hogarth.
Gellhorn, E. (1967). *Principles of autonomic-somatic integrations.* Minneapolis: University of Minnesota Press.
Gendlin, E. (1981). *Focusing.* New York: Everest House.
Goleman, D. (1971). Meditation as meta-therapy: Hypothesis towards a proposed fifth state of consciousness. *Journal of Transpersonal Psychology, 3,* 1–25.
Guidano, V. F., & Liotti, G. (1983). *Cognitive processes and emotional disorders: A structural approach to psychotherapy.* New York: Guilford.
Heide, F. J., & Borkovec, T. D. (1983). Relaxation-induced anxiety: paradoxical anxiety enhancement due to relaxation training. *Journal of Consulting and Clinical Psychology, 51,* 171–182.
Heide, F. J., & Borkovec, T. D. (1984). Relaxation-induced anxiety: Mechanisms and theoretical implications. *Behaviour Research and Therapy, 22,* 1–12.
Hess, W. R. (1957). *The functional organization of the diencephalon.* New York: Grune & Stratton.
Hilgard, E. R. (1977). *Divided consciousness: Multiple controls in human thought and action.* New York: Wiley.
Hilgard, E. R., & Hilgard, J. R. (1975). *Hypnosis and the relief of pain.* Los Altos, CA: William Kaufmann.
Holmes, D. S. (1984). Meditation and somatic arousal reduction: a review of the experimental evidence. *American Psychologist, 39,* 1–10.
Holmes, D. S. (1985a). To meditate or to simply rest, that is the question: A response to the comments of Shapiro. *American Psychologist, 41,* 722–725.
Holmes, D. S. (1985b). To meditate or rest? The answer is rest. *American Psychologist, 40,* 728–731.
Holmes, D. S. (1987). The influence of meditation versus rest on physiological arousal: A second examination. In M. A. West (Ed.) *The Psychology of meditation,* pp. 81–103. London: Oxford.
Hull, C. L. (1943). *Principles of behavior.* New York: Appleton-Century-Crofts.
Ikemi, Y., Ishikawa, H., Goyeche, J. R. M., & Sasaki, Y. (1978). Positive and negative aspects of the altered states of consciousness induced by autogenic training, Zen and yoga. *Psychotherapy and Psychosomatics, 30,* 170–178.
Iyengar, B. K. S. (1965). *Light on yoga.* New York: Schocken Books.
Iyengar, B. K. S. (1981). *Light on pranayama.* New York: Crossroad.
Jacobson, E. (1929). *Progressive relaxation.* Chicago: University of Chicago Press.
Jacobson, E. (1938). *Progressive relaxation* (2nd ed.) Chicago: University of Chicago Press.

James, W. (1902). *The varieties of religious experience.* New York: Modern Library.

Jung, C. G. (1976). The symbolic life. In *Collected works,* Vol 18. Princeton: Princeton University Press. (Originally published 1935).

Kanner, A. D., Coyne, J. C., Schaefer, C., & Lazarus, R. S. (1981). Comparisons of two modes of stress measurement: Daily hassles and uplifts versus major life events. *Journal of Behavioral Medicine, 4,* 1–39.

Kapleau, P. (1965). *The three pillars of Zen.* Boston: Beacon.

Kelly, G. A. (1955). *The psychology of personal constructs.* New York: Norton.

Kohr, R. L. (1984). Dimensionality in meditative experiences: A replication. in D. H. Shapiro & R. H. Walsh (Eds.), *Meditation: Classic and contemporary perspectives,* pp. 271–280. New York: Aldine.

Layman, E. M. (1976). *Buddhism in America.* Chicago: Nelson-Hall.

Lazarus, R. S. (1966). *Psychological stress and the coping process.* New York: McGraw-Hill.

Lazarus, R. S., Folkman, S. (1984). *Stress, appraisal, and coping.* New York: Springer.

Lehrer, P. M. (1978). Psychophysiological effects of progressive relaxation in anxiety neurotic patients and of progressive relaxation and alpha feedback in non-patients. *Journal of Consulting and Clinical Psychology, 46,* 389–404.

Lehrer, P. M., & Woolfolk, R. L. (1984). Are stress reduction techniques interchangeable, or do they have specific effects?: A review of the comparative empirical literature. In R. L. Woolfolk & P. M. Lehrer (Eds.), *Principles and practice of stress management,* pp. 404–477. New York: Guilford.

Lesh, T. V. (1970). Zen meditation and the development of empathy in counselors. *Journal of Humanistic Psychology, 10,* 75–85.

Ley, R. & Walker, H. (1973). Effects of carbon dioxide-oxygen inhalation on heart rate, blood pressure, and subjective anxiety. *Journal of Behavior Therapy and Experimental Psychiatry, 4,* 223–228.

Lichstein, K. L. (1988). *Clinical relaxation strategies.* New York: Wiley.

Linton, H. (1983). Behavioral remediation of chronic pain: A status report. *Pain, 24,* 124–141.

Loewenfeld, L. (1901). *Der hypnotismus, handbuch der lehre von der hypnose und der suggestion.* Wiesbaden: J. F. Bergmann.

Luiselli, J. K., Steinman, D. L., Marholin, D., II, & Steinman, W. M. (1981). Evaluation of progressive muscle relaxation with conduct-problem, learning-disabled children. *Child Behavior Thearpy, 3,* 41–55.

Luthe, W. (Ed.). (1969–1973). *Autogenic therapy,* Vols. 1–6. New York: Grune & Stratton.

Luthe, W. (1965). Autogenic training in North America. In W. Luthe (Ed.), *Autogenic training: International edition,* pp. 71–78. New York: Grune & Stratton.

Luthe, W. (1977). *Stress and self-regulation: Introduction to the methods of autogenic therapy.* Pointe-Claire, Quebec: International Institute of Stress.

Mahoney, M. J. (1974). *Cognition and behavior modification.* Cambridge, MA: Ballinger.

Maliszewski, M., Twemlow, S. W., Brown, D. P., & Angler, J. M. (1981). A phenomenological typology of intensive meditation. *ReVision, 4,* 3–27.

Markus, H. (1977). Self-schmata and processing information about the self. *Journal of Personality and Social Psychology, 35,* 63–78.

Marty, M. E. (1986). *Modern American religion, Vol 1: The irony of it all.* Chicago: University of Chicago Press.

Marzuk, P. (1985). Biofeedback for hypertension: A position paper of the Health and Public Policy Committee, American College of Physicians. *Annals of Internal Medicine, 102*, 709–715.

Maslow, A. H. (1971). *The farther reaches of human nature.* New York: Viking.

Masters, R., & Houston, J. (1972). *Mind games.* New York: Dell.

Maupin, E. W. (1965). Individual differences in response to a Zen meditation exercise. *Journal of Consulting Psychology, 28*, 139–145.

Meichenbaum, D. (1977). *Cognitive-behavior modification: An integrative approach.* New York: Plenum.

Meichenbaum, D. (1985). *Stress Inoculation Training,* New York: Pergamon.

Mullen, R. E. (1986). *Handbook of cognitive therapy techniques.* New York: W. W. Norton.

Norton, G. R., Rhodes, L., & Hauch, J. & Kaprowy, E. A. (1985). Characteristics of subjects experiencing relaxation and relaxation-induced anxiety. *Journal of Behavior Therapy and Experimental Psychiatry, 16*, 211–216.

Orme-Johnson, D. W., & Farrow, J. T. (Eds.) (1977). *Scientific research on the transcendental meditation program: Collected papers* (Vol 1). Livingston Manor, NY: Maharishi European Research Universtiy Press.

Ornstein, R. (1972). *The psychology of consciousness.* San Francisco: W. F. Freeman.

Osis, K. Bokert, E., Carlson, M. L. (1973). Dimensions of the meditative experience. *Journal of Transpersonal Psychology, 5*, 109–135.

Paul, G. L. (1966, September). The specific control of anxiety: "Hypnosis" and "conditioning." In L. Oseas (Chair), *Innovations in therapeutic interactions.* Symposium presented at the meeting of the American Psychological Association, New York.

Patel, C. (1984). Yogic therapy. In R. L. Woolfolk & P. M. Lehrer (Eds.) *Principles and practice of stress management,* pp. 70–107. New York: Guilford.

Pavlov, I. (1927). *Conditioned reflexes.* Oxford, England: Oxford University Press.

Pekala, R. J. (1987). The phenomenology of meditation. In M. A. West (Ed.) *The psychology of meditation,* pp. 59–80. Oxford: Clarendon.

Pekala, R. J., & Levine, R. L. (1981). Mapping states of consciousness via an empirical-phenomenological approach. *Imagination, Cognition, and Personality, 1*, 29–47.

Pekala, R. J., Wenger, C. F., & Levine, R. L. (1985). Individual differences in phenomenological experience: States of consciousness as a function of absorption. *Journal of Personality and Social Psychology, 48*, 125–132.

Peper, E., Ancoli, S., & Quinn, M. (Eds.) (1979), *Mind/body integration.* New York: Plenum.

Poppen, R., & Maurer, J. P. (1982). Electromyographic analysis of relaxed postures. *Biofeedback and Self-Regulation, 7*, 491–498.

Prabhavananda, S. (1963). *The spiritual heritage of India.* Garden City, NY: Doubleday.

Prabhavananda, S. (1968). *Religion in practice.* Hollywood, CA: Vedanta.

Rama, Ballentine, R., & Ajaya. (1976). *Yoga and psychotherapy: The evolution of consciousness.* Glenview, IL: Himalayan Institute.

Rama, Ballentine, R., & Hymes, A. (1979). *Science of breath: A practical guide.* Honesdale, PN: Himalayan Institute.

Reed, S. D., Katkin, E. S., & Goldband, S. (1987). Biofeedback and behavioral medicine. In F. H. Kanfer & A. P. Goldstein (Eds.), *Helping People Change*, pp. 381–436. New York: Pergamon.

Reyher, J. (1964). Brain mechanisms, intrapsychic processes and behavior: A theory of hypnosis and psychopathology. *American Journal of Clinical Hypnosis, 1*, 107-119.

Roberts, A (1985). Biofeedback: Research, training, and clinical roles. *American Psychologist, 40*, 938–941.

Russo, D. C., Bird, B. L., & Masek, B. J. (1980). Assessment issues in behavioral medicine. *Behavioral Assessment, 2*, 1–18.

Russell, R. K. & Matthews, C. O. (1975). Cue-controlled relaxation in *in vivo* desensitization of a snake phobia. *Journal of Behavior Therapy and Experimental Psychiatry, 6*, 49–51.

Samuels, M., & Samuels, N. (1975). *Seeing with the mind's eye: History, techniques, and uses of visualization.* New York: Random House.

Sarbin, T. R., & Slagle, R. W. (1979). Hypnosis and psychophysiological outcomes. In E. Fromm, & R. E. Shor (Eds.). *Hypnosis: Developments in research and new perspectives (2nd ed.)*, pp 273–303. New York: Aldine.

Schneider, C. J. (1987). Cost effectiveness of biofeedback and behavioral medicine treatments: A review of the literature. *Biofeedback and Self-Regulation, 12*, 71–92.

Schultz, J. H. (1932). Das autogene training: Konzentrative selbstent spannung (12 Auflage). Stuttgart: Georg Thieme.

Schultz, J. H. & Luthe, W. (1959). *Autogenic training: A psychophysiologic approach in psychotherapy.* New York: Grune & Stratton.

Schwartz, M. S. (1987). *Biofeedback: A practitioner's guide.* New York: Guilford.

Schwartz, G. E., Davidson, R. J., & Goleman, D. T. (1978). Patterning of cognitive and somatic processes in the self regulation of anxiety: Effects of meditation versus exercise. *Psychosomatic Medicine, 40*, 321–328.

Selye, H. (1956). *The stress of life.* New York: McGraw-Hill.

Shapiro, D. H. (1980). *Meditation.* Chicago: Aldine.

Shapiro, D. H. (1984). Classic perspectives of meditation: Toward an empirical understanding of meditation as an altered state of consciousness. In D. H. Shapiro & R. N. Walsh (Eds.). *Meditation: Classic and contemporary approaches*, pp 12–23. New York: Aldine.

Shapiro, D. H. (1985). Clinical use of meditation as a self-regulation strategy: comments on Holmes's conclusion and implications. *American Psychologist, 40*, 719–722.

Shapiro, D. H., & Walsh, R. N. (1984). *Meditation: Classic and contemporary approaches.* New York: Aldine.

Shor, R. E., & Orne, E. C. (1962). *Harvard Group Scale of Hypnotic Susceptibility.* Palo Alto, CA: Consulting Psychologists Press.

Skinner, B. F. (1938). *The behavior of organisms.* New York: Appleton-Century-Crofts.

Siebert, J. R. (1985). *Absorption and meditation.* Unpublished master's thesis, Roosevelt University, Chicago.

Silver, B., & Blanchard, E. (1978). Biofeedback or relaxation training in the treatment of psychophysiologic disorders: Or, are the machines really necessary? *Journal of Behavioral Medicine, 1*, 217–239.

Simonton, O. C., Matthews-Simonton, S., & Creighton, J. (1978). *Getting well again.* Los Angeles: J. P. Tarcher.

Singer, J. L. (1975). *The inner world of daydreaming.* New York: Harper & Row.

Smith, J. C. (1978). Personality correlates of continuation and outcome in meditation and erect sitting control treatments. *Journal of Consulting and Clinical Psychology, 46,* 272–279.

Smith, J. C. (1986a). *Meditation: A sensible guide to a timeless discipline.* Champaign, IL: Research Press.

Smith, J. C. (1986b). Meditation, biofeedback, and the relaxation controversy: A cognitive-behavioral perspective. *American Psychologist, 41,* 1007–1009.

Smith, J. C. (1987). Meditation as psychotherapy: A new look at the evidence. In M. A. West (Ed.), *Psychology of meditation,* pp. 136–149. London: Oxford.

Smith, J. C. (1989). *Relaxation dynamics: A cognitive-behavioral approach to relaxation.* Champaign, IL: Research Press.

Smith, J. C., & Seidel, J. M. (1982). The factor structure of self-reported physical stress reactions. *Biofeedback and Self-Regulation, 7,* 35–47.

Smith, J. C., & Sheridan, M. (1983). Type A (coronary-prone) behavior and self-reported physical and cognitive reaxtions. *Perceptual and Motor Skills, 56,* 545–546.

Smith, J. C., & Siebert, J. R. (1984). Self-reported physical stress reactions: First- and second-order factors. *Biofeedback and Self-Regulation, 9,* 215–227.

Spielberger, C. D., Gorsuch, R. L., & Lushene, R. E. (1970). *State-Trait Anxiety Inventory.* Palo Alto, CA: Consulting Psychologists Press.

Staff. (1983, September 5). *Time,* p. 2.

Stone, D. (1976). The human potential movement. In C. Y. Glock, & R. N. Bellah (Eds.). *The new religious consciousness,* pp. 93–115. Berkeley, CA: University of California Press.

Stroebel, C. E. (1983). *Quieting reflex training for adults.* New York: BMA Audio Cassettes.

Suler, J. R. (1985). Meditation and somatic arousal: A comment on Holmes's review. *American Psychologist, 40,* 717.

Tart, C. T. (1967). Psychedelic experiences associated with a novel hypnotic procedure, mutual hypnosis. *American Journal of Clinical Hypnosis, 10 (2),* 65–78.

Tart, C. T. (1969). *Altered states of consciousness.* New York: Wiley.

Tart, C. T. (1970). Self-report scales of hypnotic depth. *International Journal of Clinical and Experimental Hypnosis, 18 (2),* 105–125.

Tart, C. T. (1972). Measuring the depth of an altered state of consciousness, with particular reference to self report scales of hypnotic depth. In E. Fromm & R. Shor (Eds.) *Hypnosis: Research developments and perspectives.* Chicago: Aldine.

Tart, C. T. (1975). *States of consciousness.* New York: Dutton.

Tart, C. T. (1987). *Waking up.* Boston: New Science Library.

Tellegen, A., & Atkinson, G. (1974). Openness to absorbing and self-altering experiences ("absorption"), a trait related to hypnotic susceptibility. *Journal of Abnormal Psychology, 83,* 268–277.

Van Nuys, D. (1973). Meditation, attention, and hypnotic susceptibility: A correlational study. *International Journal of Clinical and Experimental Hypnosis, 21,* 59–69.

Wallace, R. K. (1970). Physiological effects of transcendental meditation. *Science, 167,* 1751–1754.

Wallace, R. K., & Benson, H. (1972). The physiology of meditation. *Scientific American, 226,* 84–90.

Wallace, R. K., Benson, H., & Wilson, K. (1971). A wakeful hypometabolic physiologic state. *American Journal of Physiology, 221*, 795–799.

Weinstein, M., & Smith, J. C. (1989). Isometric Squeeze Relaxation (progressive relaxation) vs. meditation: Focusing, absorption, and anxiety as predictors and outcomes. Submitted for publication.

Weitzenhoffer, A. M., & Hilgard, E. R. (1962). *Stanford Hypnotic Susceptibility Scale, Form C.* Palo Alto, CA: Consulting Psychologists Press.

West, M. A. (1985). Meditation and somatic arousal reduction. *American Psychologist, 40*, 717–719.

West, M. A. (1987). *The psychology of meditation.* London: Oxford.

Wideman, M. V., & Singer, J. S. (1984). The role of psychological mechanisms in preparation for childbirth. *American Psychologist, 39*, 1357–1371.

Wilber, E., Engler, J., & Brown, J. P. (Eds.) (1986). *Transformations of counsciousness.* Boston: New Science Library.

Wolberg, L. R. (1948). *Medical hypnosis,* Vols. 1 and 2. New York: Grune & Stratton.

Wolpe, J. (1958). *Psychotherapy by reciprocal inhibition.* Stanford: Stanford University Press.

Wolpe, J. (1973). *The practice of behavior therapy* (2nd ed.) Elmsford, NY: Pergamon Press.

Woolfolk, R. L. (1975). Psychophysiological correlates of meditation. *Archives of General Psychiatry, 32*, 1326–1333.

Woolfolk, R. L., & Lehrer, P. M. (1984). *Principles and practice of stress management.* New York: Guilford.

Zinberg, N. E. (1977).The study of conscious states: Problems and progress. In N. E. Zinberg (Ed.) *Alternate states of consciousness*, pp. 1–36. New York: The Free Press.

INDEX